THE SICK SOCIETY

BY THE SAME AUTHOR

*The Political Economy of International Oil
and the Underdeveloped Countries*

By MICHAEL TANZER

HOLT, RINEHART AND WINSTON
CHICAGO   NEW YORK   SAN FRANCISCO

THE SICK
SOCIETY

an economic examination

Library of Congress Catalog Card Number: 75-138879
First Edition

Designer: Berry Eitel
SBN: 03-086018-0
Printed in the United States of America

Brief portions of this work have appeared previously in *The Nation*
and *Canadian Dimension*.

TO DEBORAH

I wish to express my gratitude to a number of people who read all or part of this manuscript and made helpful suggestions: Mary Clemmey, Chester Hartman, Harry Magdoff, Sig Moglen and Benedict Wolf. Most of all, this book has benefited greatly from innumerable discussions over the years with my wife, Dr. Deborah Tanzer. Her background as an economics major at Radcliffe College, a law student at Harvard Law School, and a graduate student in psychology at Brandeis University, has been a foil and complement to my own experience. To my sons, David and Kenneth, my thanks for the inspiration they gave simply by being themselves.

M.T.

CONTENTS

PREFACE

The original and early economists—the mercantilists, Adam Smith, Ricardo, Marx—were men not only of intelligence but also of wide learning. The breadth of view and comprehensiveness of approach that characterized these "worldly philosophers," to use Robert Heilbroner's felicitous phrase, was reflected in the fact that originally the subject was called "political economy." The lasting impact of these thinkers is irrefutable evidence that economic analysis need not be, as currently viewed, a narrow approach bordering on engineering and irrelevant to complex human problems.

In our own day the economist has become a narrowly trained and specialized technician. On the one hand we have the "theoretician," who is a logician able to manipulate a series of hypotheses with little interest in the validity of the underlying assumptions, i.e., little interest in the real world. On the other hand the "practical" economists are largely "econometricians," whose main concern, too frequently, is finding statistical relationships between different economic variables, regardless of either the causality involved in the relationships or, more important, the significance in the real world of the particular economic variables.

A few economists have resolutely resisted these trends toward sterility in economics. Among them are Paul Sweezy and the late Paul Baran; readers of their book, *Monopoly Capital,* will recognize their influence on my own approach. A more widely known maverick is John K. Galbraith, who has always attempted to deal with the broad problems facing society. The profession's disdain for this approach is indicated in an article, "The New Potentates Rule by the Numbers," which notes that although "John Kenneth Galbraith stirs the profession in spite of itself every time he publishes a book . . . the majority opinion seems to be that Galbraith is more like a modern Thorstein Veblen (big on insight, small on science) than a modern Keynes."

The present book is conceived in this neglected tradition of using economics or "political economy" as an organizing principle. The times seem particularly ripe for such an effort. The American body politic has been so convulsed in recent years that the question of whether or not this is a "sick society" has been elevated to respectability. Yet, even the sensitive and agonized citizen too often has been distracted from any fundamental examination. The events at Watts, Mylai, and the Wisconsin University Mathematics Building—the shocking symptoms of the diseases wracking America—generally have been viewed as if they were the basic diseases themselves.

More perceptive observers have recognized these eruptions as manifestations of deeper ills. Yet even then what is missing is an examination of society's fundamental anatomical deformities that both generate these diseases and make them incurable without radical surgery. This book, therefore, attempts to point out and document what prevailing liberal ideology denies—that our major social ills are not temporary historical "accidents," but are permanent and predictable outgrowths of a misshapen and inevitably malfunctioning social body.

Only such an examination can help us to understand and transcend the inadequacy of liberal prescriptions. The progressive deterioration of the American social body is inducing a fevered and nightmarish reality that is the direct enemy of the American dream. If we are ever to conceive a healthy society in which the dream and the reality are one, an accurate diagnosis is required. In this revitalization, economic analysis must recapture its historic role as a major *social* science.

ANATOMY OF
THE PATIENT

1

THE

CORPORATE ECONOMY

In this book an attempt is made to analyze the economic roots of fundamental problems currently facing American society. These problems are: (1) Vietnam, as part of the more general issue of U.S. involvement in the underdeveloped world, (2) the gold and dollar crises that hinge on our relations with the developed world, (3) racial discrimination and black poverty, and (4) a spreading sense of malaise or alienation, particularly among youth and intellectuals.

Of these four clusters of problems, the conventional wisdom of academia would view Vietnam as "political," the international monetary crises as "economic," racial discrimination as "social," and alienation as "psychological." In contrast, this book contends that there is an overriding common denominator to these problems. This is not simply the generally recognized surface interrelationships (e.g.

that the Vietnam War diverts funds from solving the racial problem), but, much more important, the common underlying economic roots and causes of these problems.

I shall provide evidence of this in the following chapters. First, however, I wish to state my initial premise more sharply. The economic roots that I am referring to are the organization and control of economic life by large profit-seeking corporations run for the benefit of the tiny upper-income elite that owns them; this economic totality I call the "corporate economy."

At this point in history it is hardly necessary to give facts proving that large corporations dominate U.S. economic life. To clear the ground for my more controversial theses, however, I quote from a recent book, *Three Faces of Power,* by A. A. Berle; Mr. Berle is the dean of the experts on the modern corporation, and one who feels that "corporate power has served the United States well":

Agriculture aside, most of the business of the United States, where it is not carried on by the government, is carried on by corporations—to be specific, about 1,200,000 of them, big and small. But four-fifths or more of the total activity is carried on by about 3,500 corporations in all. . . . Far and away the major part of the American supply-and-exchange system is constituted of a few hundred (at most) clusters of corporate enterprises, each of whose major decisions are determined by a central giant.

While the facts of corporate power are hardly disputable, I want to make it clear from the outset that I do *not* propose a "conspiracy theory" of a group of "evil corporations" that have set out to control American life. Rather, my view of the corporate economy stresses the relatively "accidental," but not unpredictable, results of the uncoordinated activities of separate firms, each having one narrow aim: profit maximization. Put another way, the corporation is here viewed as a collection of ordinary, inherently decent men and women whose job it is to make the most possible money for the company. If the results of this endeavor, owing to the interactions among corporations and between the corporate world and the outside society as a whole, are. not what the individuals themselves might have desired, this is clearly not their fault. Thus, one of the central themes of this analysis is that the corporate economy as a whole is bigger than and different from its individual components, considered either separately or as an arithmetical aggregate.

Nevertheless, another key theme is that corporate activities and participation in the corporate world leave their mark on the individual and his psychology. People cannot work in institutions whose activities differ from their personal desires without it affecting their own personalties. Anyone who has worked in the corporate world for any length of time has seen in others, and may have developed in himself, a defensive mechanism for rationalizing the gaps between his values and the actions of his corporation. This rationalization, nicely summarized in that aphorism, "Well, business is business" (a more defensive Eichmannian variant of which is, "Well, I only work here") itself reflects the widespread psychological alienation found *within* the corporation.

Furthermore, while I assume a general unity in the corporate view, individual corporations are not seen as acting in unison or even necessarily as having the same interests in major problems. Hence, this is not a theory of a "ruling class" elected by the board of directors of each major corporation to run a society. In fact, individual corporations are frequently quite competitive with each other, and the tension between monopoly and competition within industries and across industries is one of the basic determinants of the course of American economic life. Thus, in relation to major economic issues it is probably safer to speak of an "industry view" than a "corporate view," e.g., it is far more likely that all the leading oil companies (or their executives) will have a similar position on the Vietnam War than will Boeing and Polaroid. To the extent that there tends to be a unified corporate view on crucial problems, this stems from the general conditioning received by all individuals operating within profit-maximizing corporations, reinforced by the various corporations popularly known as the "mass media": e.g., Columbia Broadcasting System, *Inc.,* The New York Times, *Inc.,* Metro-Goldwyn-Mayer, *Inc.,* Time, *Inc.,* etc.

The modern corporation is basically an intricate mechanism for harnessing thousands of people's efforts toward the single overriding goal of long-run profit maximization. By and large the beneficiaries of the corporation's activities are its stockholders. But, who are these stockholders? According to the latest survey of the New York Stock Exchange, they number over 30 million Americans. Before, however, one accepts this as proof of the widely ballyhooed "people's capitalism," it is necessary to take a closer look at the distribution of this stock among the 30 million people.

There are no definitive data publicly available, but Robert J. Lampman, whose own pioneering study covering the 1922-53 period is the most authoritative source, notes that, "All studies of stock ownership indicate that this asset is highly concentrated." Lampman estimates that in 1953 at least four-fifths of all corporate stock was owned by the top 1 percent of wealth holders (those with assets of at least $60,000, or some 1.5 million people). Even more, his detailed data indicate that the richest of the rich, the top 5 percent of this upper 1 percent, owned half of this group's stock. Thus, 75,000 adults, each with total assets of $500,000 or more, owned at least 40 percent of all the corporate stock in the entire country! Moreover, corporate stock accounted for 35 percent of all the assets of the wealthiest 1 percent, but for the "upper 75,000," corporate stock represented over 55 percent of their total wealth. There is no evidence that this situation has changed radically in the last two decades. (In fact, Lampman's estimates for 1922-53 indicate, if anything, a rising concentration of stock ownership.) Overall then, it seems fair to conclude that the modern corporation clearly represents the vehicle of a tiny economic elite for protecting and furthering its own economic interests.

It is crucial for understanding the true nature of society today to recognize—and realizing its full implications accept—that the overriding goal of the modern corporation is profit maximization. For decades economists had no doubt on this question. But in recent years, with the growth of various brands of a "managerial revolution" theory, a confusion has developed, not only in the public's mind but also in the mind of the professional economist. This confusion began in the 1930s, when Berle and Means put forth the theory that there had been a "divorce" between ownership and management of the modern corporation. As a result, so goes the theory, the modern "managerial class" does not necessarily have to maximize profits, but can also pursue social goals: the modern corporation can have a "soul." As expressed recently by an academic specialist in business-society relations:

In contrast to the traditional businessman, the manager sees himself as a steward of the public interest. He thinks of his role as that of a mediator between the various and often opposing interest groups that make up the firm and its environment—stockholders, workers, customers, competitors, and the government. Such a role requires that he stress the values of cooperation and organizational ability more than the traditional businessman would.

The theory's attractiveness stems from its partial grounding in fact. Over the last half century there has been a trend toward transfer of direct operating control of major businesses from the personal supervision of the owners to that of a hired professional managerial group. The epitome of this might be the shift in operating control of Standard Oil of New Jersey from John D. Rockefeller to a sixteen-man board of directors—a board with over four-hundred years of collective experience in the oil industry.

The fault with the managerial revolution theory is that it leaps from the fact that ownership is no longer synonymous with active control of operations to the conclusion that the managers of large corporations no longer place decisive weight on profit maximization. From this author's wide experience in the corporate world, including working for Standard Oil of New Jersey, this clearly does not follow in practice.

Evidence for my view is contained in a recent study of the statistical relationship between type of control and rate of profit in major corporations. The study found that where there was a change from nonmanagement control to management control, "this had a favorable influence on the profit rate," and concluded: "This result is in sharp contrast to the usual hypothesis, implicit in almost all the new theories of the firm that suggest that the increasing separation of ownership and management should be associated with less emphasis on profit maximization and more on other goals."

Even without this kind of statistical evidence, there would be good reason for assuming that the management controlled corporation must be vitally interested in profits. For one thing, profits are a crucial factor in determining whether over the long run a corporation grows, stagnates, or dies. Profits provide the wellspring for new plants and equipment, support product research and development, make possible acquisitions of markets and sources of raw materials, enable diversifications into new industries, and yield liquid resources for cushioning against bad times or seizing on new opportunities. All of these allow the corporation to maintain or improve its competitive position vis-à-vis other firms in the same industry, other industries, and foreign firms, while at the same time allowing management maximum freedom of action. Particularly as international competition increases, or the business cycle turns down, firms that fall behind in the profits race imperil both their long-run viability and management's room for maneuvering. On the other hand, firms that have been profit leaders can take advantage of adversity. Clearly the professional manager has a parallel interest with corporate stockholders in seeing that his firm is among the winners rather than among the losers.

For another thing, there is no simple cleavage between owners and managers of corporations because managers have an important personal ownership stake in their companies. It is true that officers and directors of large corporations generally own only a small percentage of their companies' stock. Unfortunately, this has been widely misinterpreted as evidence that management's personal incomes are largely insulated from those of their companies. In point of fact, even though the managers of a corporation may hold a relatively small share of its stock, this amount is often a relatively large share of their personal assets. Given this, their goals are directly linked to those of the company's stockholders.

To cite a specific example of a company classically considered as "management-controlled," in 1969 Standard Oil of New Jersey's twenty-five directors and officers collectively owned 125,000 shares of its stock, and had options to buy another 250,000 shares. In total, these 375,000 shares represented less than .2 of 1 percent of all of Jersey's stock. However, the $30 million market value of these management shares was fifteen times as great as the managers' annual salaries and bonuses. Moreover, since capital gains on stock receive highly preferential tax treatment over salaried income, possible increases in the market value of the company's stock would take on even greater significance for management.

Carrying the case even further, I would argue that the development of the modern managerial elite has *strengthened* rather than weakened the corporate drive toward profit maximization. Here it is necessary to distinguish between the "profit motive" as a subjective individual drive, and "profit maximization" as an objective collective goal. It may well be that owners of a family corporation have a stronger "profit motive" than the managerial elite, since the owner derives most of his direct income from profits while the manager derives most of his from salary. On the other hand, the owner can also be more "generous" or socially minded; the fact that the corporation and the individual are one will lead him to use the corporation to maximize his individual welfare, which might be at the expense of company profits. Thus, a Robert Owen (the British socialist-businessman) might pay high wages and make his factories showpieces, while a Henry Ford might undergo long strikes in order to teach his workers "a lesson," with each action being detrimental to profit maximization. The recent wage of conglomerate takeovers, discussed later, evidences the views of Eli Goldston, articulate president of the fast-growing Eastern Gas and Fuel Associates:

> The degree of separation between owners and managers of modern big business has been overstated. So has the alleged ability of incompetent or unaggressive management to survive and even to perpetuate itself by selecting its successors. . . . The firms where unaggressive management can relax are typically ones where a founding family is still powerful enough to keep control and affluent enough not to press for profit maximization. Except in such firms, ownership is proving to be an increasingly strong influence on management.

The spread of the managerially run corporation tends to eliminate the possibilities of such profit reducing aberrations. It does so both by substituting collective rule for individual rule and by making it legally and morally impermissible for management not to seek maximum profits.

Even more important, within the framework of collective decision making in the modern corporation, profit maximization is the only criterion that is relatively unambiguous, precise, and unarguable. Particularly in the competition among managers for top positions (both within and among firms), profit maximization for the stockholders is the ultimate rationale for the existence of the managerial class as well as the indisputable yardstick. Any company tolerating frequent deviations from the goal of profit maximization would wreak havoc with the morale of its modern, scientifically trained managerial group and hence tend to fall even further behind in the profit race.

These points have been simply put by Mr. Goldston:

For the new manager, the lure of personal financial gain is thus linked to that of publicized good performance; he seeks good results for reasons both of personal gain and of team pride. He realizes a significant part of his compensation through market appreciation and therefore tends to appraise his own performance, even if his functions are non-financial, by the stock exchange scoreboard that operates from 10:00 A.M. to 3:30 P.M. each market day and displays the market opinion of the management team to which he belongs. One should think of big business in the United States as something like a highly competitive professional sport in which the players have intertwined desires for greater personal wealth and for team victory. . . .

With the clear focus of business on a public scoreboard where growth in earnings per share is the major criterion, it is easy to understand that *earnings growth has become the consuming objective of American business.*

That this all-consuming goal of profit maximization may be ignored by some neophyte business practitioners hardly refutes the rule, and is done at peril to their advancement. Thus, Andrew Hacker in a perceptive article on "The Making of a (Corporation) President," passes on the view from the top:

"It's remarkable how many of the young fellows we take in go along for years without realizing that their real job is to make money for the company," one executive remarked. . . .

. . . The up-and-comer, however, soon learns to think first and foremost in business terms: the specialized skills he was taught at college are only useful if they can be applied to augmenting the firm's earnings. At a certain point he may have to compromise with professional standards in making or promoting a profitable but less-than-quality product. How he reacts to this challenge will be noted by his superiors.

Additionally, it should be noted that insofar as modern management decision-making techniques combined with computer technology make possible greater refinements in profit forecasting and measurement, it may be increasingly difficult to justify "socially responsible" corporate behavior. Thus, while today's management can give large gifts to education and to charity, the ultimate yardstick for justifying such behavior must be the "long run profit maximization" of the company. As Gaylord A. Freeman, Jr., chairman of the First National Bank of Chicago, put it, "The use of stockholders' assets to improve the society can be justified if the societal improvement redounds to the benefit of the corporation. . . . If, on the other hand, the cause is just 'a good cause,' with no prospect of enhancing future earnings, then . . . it is an unjustified gift of funds belonging to the stockholders." Thus, as market research and measurement techniques improve, it will be increasingly difficult for corporate management to do "good deeds" if they can be shown to be at the expense of profit maximization.

One little noticed aspect of the managerial revolution's refinement of corporate profit seeking is sufficiently important to deserve separate discussion. This is the rapid spread within the last ten years of profit measurement techniques that stress the frequently greater value to a firm of a bird in the hand as opposed to even two sure ones in the bush; the basic reason being that today's profits can be reinvested to make for even greater future profits. Thus, a major new innovation in computing the profitability of projected investments has been use of the "discounted cash flow" (DCF) method. The essence of this method is that it defines the profit rate of a projected investment as equal to that interest rate which, if paid by a bank on the original investment and *compounded* over the life of the project, would yield at the end the same amount of dollars as the profits projected from the investment.

The significance of this modern DCF profit calculation

method is its stress on the "time value of money." This tends to negate what has traditionally been considered one of the great virtues of the large corporations: namely, their long-range interests in situations, as opposed to the presumably short-range ambitions of smaller business attempting to make a "quick kill." On the contrary, for the large companies that dominate the U.S. economy and seek high profit rates from their monopolistic position, the modern stress on the time value of money tends to give the companies a very short-range view.

As a result, the profit calculus of modern business signals that normally it is more profitable for big corporations to plunder now and worry about the fallout later. Conversely, it gives the profit-maximizing corporation a strong tendency to defer "avoidable" costs as long as possible, since the real cost to the firm normally will be lower in the future. The implications of this for the corporate economy's likely response to today's social problems are enormous, and will be discussed later in this and other chapters.

First, however, I want to dispute a variant of the managerial revolution theory, as expressed in Galbraith's *The New Industrial State*. Galbraith's thesis is that historically economic power accrues to the scarce factor of production in an economy. In medieval times this power was in the hands of landowners, while in recent centuries it belonged to owners of capital. Now, he claims, it is not capital but "organized intelligence" that is scarce. This factor is possessed by the "technocrats," who thus have the real economic power today.

Who are these "technocrats"? Galbraith defines them as a group much larger than, but encompassing, the Berle-Means managerial elite:

[Management] is a collective and imperfectly defined entity; in the large corporation it embraces chairman, president, those vice presidents with important staff or departmental responsibility, occupants of other major staff positions and, perhaps, division or department heads not included above. It includes, however, only a small proportion of those who, as participants, contribute information to group decisions. This latter group is very large; it extends from the most senior officials of the corporation to where it meets, at the outer perimeter, the white and blue collar workers whose function is to conform more or less mechanically to instruction or routine. It embraces all who bring specialized knowledge, talent or experience to group decision-making. This, not the management, is the guiding intelligence— the brain—of the enterprise. There is no name for all who participate in group decision-making or the organization which they form. I propose to call this organization the Technostructure.

The critical point that Galbraith undervalues is the fact that the technostructure is hired and controlled by the top managerial group in the modern corporation, and in most cases cannot function outside the corporation. As Leonard Silk, former editor of *Business Week* and long-time student of corporate behavior, points out:

The prediction of a technocratic takeover was first made, of course, by Veblen in 1919; he asserted that the "technologists" were discovering that together they constitute "the indispensable General Staff of the Industrial System" and could, "in a few weeks, incapacitate the country's productive industry."
. . . Galbraith [has], I think, somewhat overstated the case. Many board chairmen and presidents are far from powerless either outside or within their own organizations, and "the technostructure" does not make the most important business decisions or provide its own leadership in corporations. As I observe corporate behavior, organizational achievements or failures are

more related to the performance of top management than to the technostructure.

American technologists are as far away today as they were fifty years ago from taking control of the American economic system or the corporations in which they are employed. Scientists or engineers customarily strive to achieve power within the business world by making themselves into *businessmen,* rather than by remaining technicians. One route that leads in the direction of genuine corporate power is through graduate work in business or executive training courses paid for by their employers, and schools of business administration endow their graduates not with the values of a new technological elite, but with the attitudes of the existing profit-oriented business management. Business management does not *fear* the technologists; it needs all sorts of specialists to solve problems not only of production, but of marketing, finance, and accounting and to cope with the corporation's labor, community, and government relations. Top management is pleased when a specialist shows that he is qualified for general managerial responsibility and has a highly developed sense of the importance of making money.

Moreover, there is no evidence that "organized intelligence" is today relatively more scarce than capital. Quite the contrary, since what gives ownership of a factor of production economic power is basically the ability to control supply, toward the goal of keeping the price of the factor high. Clearly, from Galbraith's definition of the technostructure, there are millions of people who own or possess "organized intelligence." But they are far from a unified class or group. In particular, they completely lack the ability to block entry into their ranks, either through control of the universities where their new members are born, or through control of entry into specific jobs within the corporations. After all, members of the technostructure have no unions, and new members sprout as universities, supported by business, expand largely in response to corporate needs. For example, ten years ago there was a great cry about the shortage of engineers in our society and the good living that could be made by them. As engineering salaries rose in response to this scarcity, corporations and government poured large sums of money into expanding engineering graduate schools and hundreds of thousands of students were attracted into the field. Now, in response to changing business conditions there is an oversupply of engineers.

On the other hand, while our enormously productive society has huge quantities of capital, ownership of this capital is quite concentrated. Not only is capital concentrated in the hands of the upper-income elite, but in most major industries it is concentrated in a handful of big corporations. Moreover, since in the key industries of society (e.g., automobile, oil, steel, aluminum, computer) vast quantities of capital are needed to enter and compete *effectively* with existing corporations, new entry is virtually precluded. This allows those corporations that now hold sway to generate monopolistic profits and vast quantities of new capital, which can be used either for expanding their existing business or going into new lines. Thus, while capital is abundant in terms of the existence of billions of dollars, its tight concentration in meaningfully large quantities makes big capital, which one needs for real economic power, truly scarce. After all, how many pools of several hundred million dollars, the minimum entry fee for many major industries, exist today even in the affluent society?

Finally, all the managerial revolution theories greatly underestimate the role of Wall Street in affecting corporate life. Wall Street plays a role, not as the villain of *Pravda*'s cartoons by actively running American life, but in a more impersonal way. Any corporation whose technostructure or management fails to operate it in a sufficiently profitable manner runs the grave risk of attempted take-over by the billions of dollars that are always available in or through Wall Street for a potentially highly profitable investment. The threat of the corporate raider—whether a superrich individual, a temporary combine of financial institutions with huge resources, or another major corporation—outflanking entrenched management by buying out a company's stockholders has always been an ever present threat to any corporate management paying inadequate attention to profits. The fact that until recently there have not been a large number of "take-overs" by corporate raiders does not mean that this threat has been any less real to knowledgeable management; actual raids are simply the tip of the iceberg. In the words of Eli Goldston, himself a highly successful corporate acquirer:

Not only shareholders, but institutional lenders and public creditors are intent on profitable performance, and they may bring quiet but considerable pressure, the existence or true nature of which is seldom publicly revealed. Those economists who believe that size and inertia provide a safe moat for an incompetent but incumbent management should follow Hodson's "Beauties Between the Balance Sheets" or *Finance Magazine*'s "Wolves of Wall Street," which list companies selling below break-up value. Watching the names of the listed firms disappear suggests that the moat is loaded with amphibian sharks who are not above crawling out to devour those they are intended to defend.

Any doubts about the latent threat to any management that fails to maximize profits should have been dissipated by the rash of take-overs of major firms by "conglomerate" enterprises in the late 1960s. Conglomerate corporations, like Ling-Temco-Vought, Inc., and Gulf & Western, Inc., to name two of the better known ones, were able to sky-rocket from tiny firms to billion dollar corporations by acquiring diverse companies, many of which had been relatively stagnant or unsuccessful. The usual technique was to offer common stock or bonds in the conglomerate in exchange for the shareholders' stock in these sleeping giants. The dazzling success of the conglomerates, at least for a few years, attested dramatically to the willingness, nay eagerness, of shareholders in pursuit of greater profits to sell existing management down the river. By 1968 eighty companies that were on *Fortune* magazine's 1962 list of the top five hundred industrial corporations had either completely disappeared into the maws of other corporations or come under their control.

The ultimate rationale of the new conglomerates is that their managerial skill is a unique and scarce resource; this resource can be used for improving the profits of any company a conglomerate acquires, regardless of its particular industry. Whatever the merits of this conglomerate theory, the crucial point is that it is rooted in profit maximization—the conglomerates claim they can make more money from a pile of existing assets than can the incumbent management (a claim strenuously denied by most of the latter).

The modern corporation ultimately can be seen as the logical heir to the private family business, with the increasingly complex operations of today's industry delegated to the trained hands of professional management. For this service management is amply rewarded. But despite frequently enormous salaries, bonuses, stock options, etc., the aggregate rewards of hired top management are insignificant compared to the fantastic profits generated for the owners of U.S. corporations—in recent years over $40 billion annually, after taxes. To take a sample of three major companies, at General Motors the $15 million in salary and bonuses received by its sixty-seven officers and directors is less than 1 percent of its after tax net income; at Bethlehem Steel, the remuneration of thirty-seven officers and directors was 2.5 percent of net income; at Standard Oil of New Jersey, the twenty-five officers and directors received only one quarter of 1 percent of the company's profits.

Thus, for a relatively small outlay, corporate owners have as servants a highly professional group painstakingly trained in an ethos of service to the owners through one overriding goal: profit maximization. Conservative economists particularly have expounded this as the only proper role for the modern corporation. In the words of Milton Friedman, "Few trends could so thoroughly undermine the very foundations of our free society as the acceptance by corporate officials of a social responsibility other than to make as much money for their stockholders as possible."

Indeed, the ultimate rationale of the capitalist system today is the same as that formulated so ably almost two hundred years ago by Adam Smith with his doctrine of the "invisible hand":

It is not from the benevolence of the butcher, the brewer, or the baker, that we expect our dinner, but from their regard to their own interest. We address ourselves, not to their humanity but to their self-love, and never talk to them of our own necessities but of their advantages.

In my judgment, the Smithian view has prevailed in modern America, with disastrous implications.

Most important, the dominant institution of society is not oriented to human needs, either material or psychological. Its overwhelming stress is rather on people as monetary costs and potential consumers, with the corporation's success depending on its ability to minimize costs while maximizing sales. On the cost side, Marx's concept of workers as labor power, or ability to work, is still the best expression of the corporate view of workers. This can be seen clearly in an industry like automobile production that has pioneered in assembly line mass production techniques.

The dehumanizing nature of work in this, the country's most crucial industry, was pointed up recently by *Fortune*, which noted that "The deep dislike of the job and the desire to escape become terribly clear twice each day when shifts end and the men stampede out the plant gates to the parking lots, where they sometimes actually endanger lives in their desperate haste to be gone." The same article passes on a shocking event for the corporate mentality: "Some assembly line workers are so turned off, managers report with astonishment, that they just walk away in midshift and don't even come back to get their pay for time they have worked."

On the output side, production in the corporate economy is consciously oriented solely to what can be sold profitably, rather than what is necessary or desirable for society. This approach is so fundamental as to be taken completely for granted. To take one simple illustration, market research starts with money demand, rather than human need. Thus, any executive who came into a corporate planning meeting and said, "I found a great new outlet for our breakfast cereals, the hungry poor of Kentucky," would immediately be laughed at; were he to persist he would be a strong candidate for early retirement.

That production for profit results in a very different range of output than that which would be dictated by real human needs is assured by the maldistribution of income in the sick society. In Chapter 5 I show in detail how the whims or induced desires of the middle and upper classes take precedence over the basic needs of the poor. Here let me cite one particularly horrendous example from my own experience. A number of years ago, scientists in one of the country's leading international companies happened upon a laboratory process for making a new type of fertilizer that held real promise for greatly expanding rice production. Successful development would clearly be enormously important for saving literally millions of lives throughout the underdeveloped world. When the company scientists reported the new discovery to corporate management and proposed to develop the fertilizer for this purpose, they were told to drop this approach. Instead, their scientific work was reorganized along the lines of developing the fertilizer for making greener lawn grass in the United States! The reason was that calculations showed the potential buying power of Americans desiring a more verdant lawn was far greater than that of impoverished peasants needing improved fertilizers. Thus, as soon as the data pointed out the correct direction for profit maximization, corporate management redirected the technostructure's work to meet that goal.

In general, the public sectors—health, education, culture, recreation, care of the aged, welfare—all are given short shrift because they do not clearly redound to the net benefit of corporations. Ultimately all of these involve some form of income redistribution channeled through government taxes and expenditures. For the corporate sector, these things are viewed as primarily causing higher taxes while providing insufficient benefits to offset these taxes. For example, a $1 billion government health program would cost a company like General Motors, which pays 2 percent of all U. S. taxes, $20 million. Given GM's current 14 percent profit margin on sales, such a government program would have to increase its sales by $140 million in order for the company to "break even." Such an increase is hardly likely. However, a billion-dollar federal highway program is obviously a horse of a different color.

Society also suffers under corporate domination because the philosophy of private profit maximization becomes embedded in the public sector. To take one important example, government policy toward housing, the president's Council of Economic Advisors reports that "Investing in new housing for low-income families—particularly in big cities—is usually a losing proposition. Indeed, the most profitable investment is often one that demolishes the homes of low-income families to make room for businesses and higher-income families." As Michael Harrington aptly comments:

It is obvious that the criterion of profitability to which the Council refers is private since, as the gloomy projections of the Violence Commission demonstrate, the social cost of the present system is bankrupting the society. Yet precisely this private calculus is the one the government follows. As the Urban Problems Commission put it, ". . . renewal was and is too often looked upon as a federally financed gimmick to provide relatively cheap land for a miscellany of profitable or prestigious enterprises."

In a society based on class inequality and suffused with commercial values, it just doesn't "make sense" to waste resources on social uses or beauty—or anything that cannot be quantified in dollars and cents. Our legislators, drawn almost exclusively from the middle and upper classes, cannot bring themselves to forget those principles that are sacred to a private economy. To them it seems logical to invest the federal dollar in undertakings that run the lowest risk and will show the highest and most immediate return.

The other side of the coin is the irresponsibility of the individual corporation toward the social problems it generates. Some of these problems are now in the public eye, for example, the common corporate decision to have minimum cost waste disposal by polluting the water and the air. While this is much decried by the environmentalists, few voices are raised against the irrationality of periodic widespread unemployment that blights people's lives and spirits and may be an even more serious aspect of built-in corporate irresponsibility to social problems.

The simple fact is that when the economy begins to turn down and a corporation's sales and profits shrink, there is no choice for the profit-maximizing corporation but to lay off workers. This is true even though virtually everyone accepts the Keynesian message that this will simply worsen the overall situation. Unemployed auto workers cannot buy houses which means there will be layoffs of construction workers who then cannot buy autos, and that means further unemployment among auto workers, and so on in a vicious downward spiral.

The heart of the problem is that no single corporation or group of corporations, no matter how large, can break the spiral. Even if the entire auto industry agreed not to lay off workers as a result of its declining sales, as long as the rest of the corporate sector was cutting back on employment, the profits of the auto corporations would be reduced as a result of their socially responsible behavior. The structural situation is analogous to a town of a thousand people guarded by a dike that suddenly springs a thousand different leaks. Unless everyone can be sure that everyone else will put his finger in a hole, the rational policy is to be the first to run like hell. Because there is no mechanism to guarantee individual responsibility within the corporate sector, the bursting dam is inevitable.

The conventional wisdom sees the solution to these problems of corporate irresponsibility as lying in "Big Brother Government" providing the coordination and compulsion necessary to prevent the corporate economy from wreaking large-scale damage. In my view this faith is misplaced. Government efforts to force solution of the long-range problems like pollution and decrepit housing normally involve high costs to the corporate sector, whether directly through investment in nonpolluting waste disposal, or indirectly through taxes for government housing subsidies. Therefore, the corporate sector uses all of its great power in the political arena to minimize government efforts in these areas.

Following the dictates of profit maximization which stress that a dollar saved today is worth two dollars five years from now, even where public pressure is so great that the corporate sector cannot block some changes, it modifies the old adage to "if you can't beat them, join them —*slowly*." Thus, there is a strong tendency for governmental remedies to fall further and further behind the growing problems. For example, despite twenty-five years of a governmental commitment to low income public housing, according to a recent presidential commission report, ". . . over the last decades, government action through urban renewal, highway programs, demolitions on public housing sites, code enforcement, and other programs has destroyed more housing for the poor than government at all levels has built for them."

With regard to the life-and-death problem for the corporate sector of threatened economic bust, in principle it is more willing to see "Big Brother" swing into action. Here the basic problem is that for a variety of reasons, which I discuss later, our current economic problems that could culminate in an economic collapse are of such a fast-moving nature as to make it impossible for government to move quickly enough to stem the deluge. To take one illustration indicative of the time problem, a major corporation like the Penn Central Railroad can suddenly be thrust into bankruptcy over a weekend, while its reorganization under governmental jurisdiction may take from ten to twenty years.

One other aspect of the deleterious effects on human life of a society dominated by socially irresponsible corporations merits mention. At least in theory American political democracy can offer some protection to our citizens from corporate irresponsibility. However, in the world of sovereign nations there is little shield for the weak and the poor countries from the depredations of the ever expanding American corporate empire. Certainly, the dog-eat-dog philosophy inculcated in Americans by the corporate credo of profit maximization and competition is not conducive to serious concern for their welfare. Given the enormous power of the sick society in the world today, "free competition" on a world scale is no more than the fox's self-serving cry of "every man for himself" as he rampages in the chicken coop.

Having completed our examination of the basic structure and logic of the corporate economy, at least one point should be clear. In order to assess its influence on some of the key problems of the sick society, as well as the possibilities of overcoming these problems within the present framework, it is necessary to have a clear understanding of the corporate sector's relationships to the political structure. It is to this task that we now turn.

2

THE CORPORATE
ECONOMY AND
POLITICAL POWER

The masters of the government of the United States are the
combined capitalists and manufacturers of the United States. It
is written over every intimate page of the records of Congress,
it is written all through the history of conferences at the White
House, that the suggestions of economic policy in this country
have come from one source, not from many sources. . . .

Suppose you go to Washington and try to get at your government. You will always find that while you are politely listened
to, the men really consulted are the men who have the biggest
stake—the big bankers, the big manufacturers, the big masters
of commerce, the heads of railroad corporations and of steam-
ship corporations.

Marx? Lenin? Galbraith? No, these are the words of Woodrow Wilson, and that they still adequately describe the
relationship between the corporate economy and the
government in the United States today is attested to by

Nicholas Johnson, a member of the Federal Communications Commission:

I think basically you have to start with a realization that the country is principally run by big business for the rich. Maybe you have to live in Washington to know that and maybe everyone in the country knows it intuitively, I don't know, but a government of the people, by the people, and for the people has become, I think, a government of the people, certainly, but by the corporations and for the rich.

To appreciate the validity of such strong assertions, we must examine each major branch of government.

First, however, I want briefly to discuss a problem of methodology. By and large the intellectual community in the United States resists the concept of a ruling group or power elite. Partly their resistance derives from the frequent association of the concept with simple minded "conspiracy" theories of history. Another reason for resistance is that it is sometimes felt, perhaps subconsciously, that to identify a "ruling group" is to condemn it (perhaps thereby also inviting retribution). A final reason is that the existence of ruling groups cannot normally be demonstrated by precise data that meet academic requirements of "proof." The "ivy tower" of the academic world is a poor vantage point for understanding the key and sensitive areas of the power struggle in society. This is particularly true because the academic can only rely upon the published material available to him. (The academic mania for quantification has too often even excluded valuable qualitative material that appears in the mass media.)

The great bulk of the crucial activities of corporations as well as governments never gets into published form except in selectively shaped material put forth to provide the most favorable possible picture. Corporate and governmental personnel at all levels, but particularly near the top, are acutely aware of the dangers of putting crucial ideas, deals, and data in written form. The dangers for the corporation include unfavorable publicity, government investigations that may subpoena damaging documentation, and industrial espionage by competitors. In addition, an individual bureaucrat, corporate or government, may not wish to have the responsibility for particular ideas or data firmly placed on his shoulders, lest he be a scapegoat if events prove damaging. Hence, as anyone who has participated in the activities of the corporate bureaucracies knows, seldom are most of the determinants of crucial decisions published in the mass media—often they are not even committed to widespread distribution within the institution itself. Telephone calls (except perhaps in Washington, D.C. and in the case of extremely sensitive matters) and face to face meetings between members of the ruling group (preferably in a private social club) are far more common than discussions or debates in the mass media.

An excellent example of the dangers otherwise can be seen in the celebrated case of Julius Klein, a $150,000 a year lobbyist for West German interests, who used Senator Thomas Dodd to further his own position with his clients; Klein drafted a letter for Dodd to send to a West German Cabinet Minister, praising Klein, and wrote across the bottom: "Please destroy this letter. I made *no copy*." Unfortunately for both Dodd and Klein, Dodd did not follow these wise instructions and a copy of the letter, along with much of the rest of Dodd's files, were subsequently exposed.

By the time something gets into the mass media, it is

usually established policy that is now being transmitted to the populace. While this notion of decision making is obvious to all sophisticated "insiders," such as newspaper reporters with good connections, and is reflected in the memoirs of leaders of the ruling group, it is a notion that has had great difficulty in penetrating academic social sciences. Perhaps this is because academic social scientists are reluctant to accept the fact that key material is not available to them at the time of its greatest significance, but only at a much later date, if ever. Also, there is always the problem of trying to estimate the reliability of "insider" information. One important test is whether the claimed events are consistent with the general structure of events that can be built up from the very logic of the situation itself or corroborated by published materials. In my view one crucial test of reliability is the predictive power of the analysis that can be developed from the material, i.e., what does the analysis specifically lead us to forecast about future events? Thus, if the reader is skeptical of the structural hypothesis of corporate-government relationships discussed below, he might at least withhold judgment until our later analyses, and if still unconvinced after that, see how well it foretells the future.

Before examining the contemporary scene, it is worth noting that corporations have a long history of active involvement in American politics. For example, the seventeenth-century Virginia Company and Plymouth Company were corporations organized to promote settlement in the original colonies, and had direct political power. The beginnings of more conventional corporate political involvement go back at least to 1820, when there were about three hundred corporations in the country, concentrated in the then key economic areas of road and canal building, banking, and land development. Because at this time there was no general incorporation law, establishing a new corporation required legislative approval. Since many of the new corporations were given monopolistic privileges and direct assistance such as land grants and cash subsidies, existing corporations and would-be corporations generated tremendous political pressure in order to maintain or improve their position. In the words of one contemporary, "The bargaining and trucking away chartered privileges [corporations] is the whole business of our law makers."

By the end of the nineteenth century there were about 500,000 corporations in the United States, but the real power was concentrated in a handful of trusts that controlled such key industries as railroads, steel, and oil. Corporate control of politics was particularly blatant in that period. Thus, the Senate of 1889 was known as "the Millionaires Club," with its members including Leland Stanford of the Southern Pacific Company, Henry Payne of Standard Oil of New Jersey, George Hearst of the newspaper and mining corporations, and Chauncey Depew of the New York Central Railroad. The House of Representatives was characterized by one of its members as being "like an auction room, where more valuable considerations were disposed of under the Speaker's hammer than in any other place on earth."

Even when personal participation of business leaders in government faded, direct ties between the corporate sector and the political leadership were assured by the "systematic assessment" plan developed by leading Republican politician Mark Hanna. Under this plan corporations were to contribute to the Republican party according to their stake in the country's general prosperity and their particular regional interests; thus, to defeat the populist William Jennings Bryan, the Standard Oil Company alone donated $250,000 in 1896 to elect William McKinley.

The 1920s were a particularly favorable period for corporations, with Presidents Warren Harding and Calvin Coolidge holding views similar to those of a prominent contemporary corporate leader:

The welfare of business, especially of big business, the product of intense individualism, necessarily means the *public* welfare. The two are inseparable! . . . No citizens . . . were so well qualified to steer legislation and government as its top-notch business and professional men; none had such great interests at stake; none could judge of effective organization and transaction of public business so well as they.

While the depression of the 1930s temporarily weakened corporate influence in America, World War II required cooperation between business and government and so re-established the corporation's strong political position. With businessmen pouring into government to help run the war machine, the seeds of a very close day-to-day relationship were sown, and have lasted to this day. One indication that this was not just a temporary war time phenomenon was the mid-1950s revelation that there were over 5,000 industry committees then operating as "advisors" to the federal government.

Turning to the specific relationships between the corporate economy and the American political system, it is obvious that while the presidency is a focal point of political power, U.S. presidents have never been corporate leaders. Particularly in recent years, climbing the ladder of politics to the presidency has been virtually a full-time job demanding participation primarily in government rather than in business. Moreover, it is clear that U.S. presidents have been drawn from very varied backgrounds, ranging from the lower-middle-class heritage of Harry Truman to the patrician upbring of Franklin Roosevelt. The very fact, however, that any potential presidential candidate has normally run a long and arduous gauntlet of political jobs in lower offices is in itself significant.

Aside from this "milling" process that helps assure that mavericks do not ascend the political ladder, there are more direct mechanisms that help the corporate economy control the presidency. One of the most important is undoubtably the huge sums increasingly needed for primaries and for running in the presidential election itself. Unless the presidential aspirant is an extremely wealthy man, he must normally obtain money for an election primarily from the business community. Thus, the Republican and Democratic parties, for example, admitted spending tens of millions of dollars for the 1968 election, while the presidential primary candidates each spent millions of dollars as well. Where do these vast sums of money come from? While there is a paucity of data, for campaign contributions are a sensitive nerve in the sick society, the leading authority on the subject concludes that "overall, the bulk of American campaign activities is financed by businessmen."

Despite the fact that since 1907 corporations have been legally prohibited from contributing funds for federal elections, there is general agreement that the law has had little real impact. Only in the last few years have any corporate violators been prosecuted. Given the ingenuity of the modern corporation, many vehicles have been found for direct corporate contributions. These include purchases of blocks of tickets to fund raising dinners; supplying facilities, products or personnel as gifts or "loans"; assigning the corporation's radio or television time or advertising space to the candidate; channeling money to candidates or parties by paying inflated fees for legal, labor relations, or public relations services; giving contributions through trade associations; and purchasing "advertisements" at vastly inflated prices in special convention or anniversary brochures published by a candidate or a political party. An illustration of the potentialities of the latter technique was the 1965 Democratic publication "Toward an Age of Greatness," which cost about $100,000 to produce while generating advertisement revenues of about $1 million, much of it from corporations either regulated by or doing business with the federal government.

Finally, top corporate executives are also key contributors. In 1956, 18 percent of all "gifts" of over $500 for presidential and senatorial candidates came from officers and directors of the top 225 corporations, and averaged $2,500 each. In 1968, 300 corporate directors of the top 50 companies forming the military-industry complex donated at least $1.2 million for the election campaigns. In many cases these corporate executives are simply the vehicle for legalizing corporate contributions. In the words of a leading expert on the subject, Edwin Epstein: "Company funds frequently find their way into partisan coffers in the form of donations by executives. Bonus or salary arrangements, padded expense accounts, and the distribution of firm moneys in individual names (on occasion without the knowledge of the 'contributor') are common devices."

Lest the reader mistakenly think that this money goes exclusively to the Republican party candidate, direct contributions to Lyndon Johnson's campaign in 1964 from members of the President's Club, almost all of whom are corporate executives or their advisors, amounted to at least $4 million. Taking into account all the various vehicles of corporate contributions, Richard Barber concludes that "business picked up at least three-fourths of the tab for President Johnson's election."

While corporate money largely swung back to candidate Nixon in the 1968 election (for reasons discussed below), even top executives within certain corporations were divided. For example, the chairman of Textron, Inc. was a member of Nixon's Business Advisory Committee, while the president of Textron was a founding member of Businessmen for Humphrey-Muskie. At Ford Motor Company, Chairman Henry Ford II was a Humphrey man, Vice-President Benson Ford a Nixon supporter, and Vice-President William Clay Ford an admirer of Senator Eugene McCarthy. A "Businessmen For Humphrey-Muskie" ad placed in the *Wall Street Journal* gives a partial list of founding members and includes the president and/or chairman of the following major corporations: Archer-Daniels-Midland, Red Owl Stores, Encyclopaedia Britannica, Seagram & Sons, Celanese, McKesson and Robbins, Trans Caribbean Airways, Crown Cork & Seal, Columbia Records, City Investing, Engelhard Minerals and Chemicals, Coca Cola Export, Ford Motor, Food Fair Stores, Eastern Gas and Fuel Associates, Northwest Industries, Kaiser Industries, Avco Broadcasting, Metro-Goldwyn-Mayer, Aerojet General, National General, Braniff International, Ling-Temco-Vought, American Motors, Xerox, Kerr-McGee, Textron, Canteen, Glen Alden, Whirlpool, Admiral, Continental Air Lines, Hotel Corporation of America, Jim Walter, Pabst Brewing, and P. Lorillard.

Finally, it must not be forgotten that the corporations

ultimately toil for a relatively small number of Americans. This economic elite, whose principal assets are corporate stocks and bonds, is itself a major campaign donor. While there are no definitive data available on its campaign contributions, it is a fact of political life that the rich generally are unwilling to give their money to candidates who are antagonistic to the corporate sector.

(The fact that corporate managers and owners control the vast financial resources necessary for presidential aspirants like Hubert Humphrey and Richard M. Nixon obviously gives them considerable influence with the successful candidate. It is probably for this reason that the corporate community is leery of extremely wealthy individuals who run for office. A Kennedy can use his family's wealth to get to the top and therefore is less dependent upon the business community. This may be one reason—along with the fact that his enormous wealth is actively engaged in rivalry with other important families and constellations of corporations—that Nelson Rockefeller has been blocked from the presidency.)

Another important mechanism for corporate control of presidential candidates (as well as candidates for lower offices) is the significant position of corporate executives in state and national political parties. Again pointing out the crucial role of corporate contributions, these positions are often connected with party financing. In recent years, for example, the National Republican Finance Committee chairman was Ralph J. Cordiner, chairman of General Electric Company, while his Democratic counterpart was Arthur B. Krim, president of United Artists Corporation.

I make no claim here that the president is the servant of the business community in a "Charley McCarthy-Edgar Bergen" relationship. Any president theoretically can be a maverick, particularly if he is resigned to serving only one term in office. Even in such a case, however, there are major institutional forces that can normally stop him from doing irreparable damage in most areas of concern to the corporate community. Most obviously, of course, there is the Supreme Court, which is charged with blocking any major incursions on private property in accordance with the sacred tenets of the Constitution. Again, Congress has the power to stymie almost any presidential program for radical domestic reform, and there are strong and diverse business lobbies that provide considerable impetus to this.

One of the major mechanisms for communicating corporate views to the president is the Business Council, composed of less than one hundred leaders of the top U.S. corporations. This group has been described by one reporter as "an exclusive and self-perpetuating club of top corporate executives that had enjoyed a private and special relationship with the Government since 1933."

One indicator of the Council's power is that when an official in the Kennedy government wanted to end the *secret* nature of meetings between the Council and government leaders, Council leaders threatened to withdraw permanently, thus forcing Kennedy to backtrack and reinstate the secret meetings. It is true that Kennedy resented the imperiousness of the Council, such as their crude breach of protocol "in the troubled summer of 1963, when invited to the White House to hear Kennedy *plead* for their help in desegregation, all but two members of the Council remained seated when the president entered the East Room where they had assembled." Nevertheless, despite such frictions, evidenced also by Kennedy's famed remark, "My father always told me that all businessmen were sons of bitches," a reporter's contemporary assessment still appears pertinent: "Mr. Kennedy, in a word, was a true but not blind defender of the free enterprise system, one of the best friends that the business community ever had in the White House." (The same reporter also notes that Robert Kennedy as Attorney General was "timid rather than bold or adventuresome in anti-trust activities."

The ascendancy of Lyndon Johnson restored the close working relationship between the White House and the Business Council. When Kennedy was assassinated it was to the Council, not to the Chamber of Commerce nor the National Association of Manufacturers, that Johnson turned for industry support; later, Council members were invited to a preview of the president's State of the Union address.

Another important mechanism for corporate influence over the presidency is corporate occupancy of key cabinet positions. In the words of one writer, "A study of the Cabinets for the years 1932-1964 suggests that the power elite dominates the departments that matter most to them— State, Treasury, and Defense."

As specific illustrations, in 1952 President Eisenhower chose for Secretary of the Treasury, Business Council member George Humphrey, head of the Hanna Mining Company; for Secretary of Defense, Charles "What's good for General Motors is good for the country" Wilson, head of that company; and for Secretary of State, John Foster Dulles, a prominent corporation lawyer with important corporate connections. Similarly, President Kennedy's Secretary of the Treasury was Republican C. Douglas Dillon, head of the Wall Street investment banking firm of Dillon, Read & Company, and his Secretary of Defense was Robert McNamara, president of Ford Motor Company.

Richard Nixon's Secretary of the Treasury Kennedy is a millionaire banker and Secretary of State Rogers is a top corporate lawyer.

Furthermore, Richard Barber notes that "Many of the Cabinet and sub-Cabinet officials named by President Nixon came direct from industry, often with the clear understanding that they would return to their former employer with bonuses intact." Can the corporate community fail to get a good hearing from an assistant secretary of labor who comes to the Nixon administration straight from the executive suite of Standard Oil of New Jersey? Particularly when his stay in government is cushioned by retention of his right to collect his company bonuses and other fringe benefits plus a special $50,000 bonus to assist "in meeting expenses while with the government"?

David Horowitz has unearthed considerable material on the unofficial role of the Council on Foreign Relations in the "care and breeding of an incipient American Establishment." He reports that the Council, which excludes women and aliens, has about 1,400 members who get together in various study groups to analyze policy problems and work out positions. Businessmen, particularly from Wall Street, form the base of the Council, with the brains being furnished by top foreign policy officials and a handful of chosen academics. The financial support of the Council rests on dues, corporate contributions, revenues from its publication, *Foreign Affairs*, and grants from the major corporate foundations, particularly Rockefeller, Ford, and Carnegie.

The top leadership that oversees the work of the Council is normally from the corporate elite. Thus, in 1946, at the beginning of the Cold War, the chairman of the Council was a Morgan Bank partner and the president was

Allen Dulles, future director of the Central Intelligence Agency, who at that time was a lawyer for Standard Oil Company of New Jersey and a director of the United Fruit Company. Twenty years later the chairman was John J. McCloy, director of many corporations and former chairman of the board of Chase Manhattan Bank, and the president was Grayson Kirk, a director of Socony Mobil and head of Columbia University. The Council's vice-president was David Rockefeller, president of the Chase Manhattan Bank.

Corporate control of the Council on Foreign Relations appears to have reaped rich dividends. It is significant that one member of the Council stated: "Whatever General Eisenhower knows about economics, he learned at the study group meetings [in 1949]." Considering that the Eisenhower years were the golden age of business participation in government, this is quite a tribute to the Council. Again, when John Kennedy was making his first staff appointments, sixty-three members of the Council were among the first eighty-two names on the list prepared for him for State Department appointments. Among his ultimate choices were Council members for Secretary of State, Secretary of the Treasury, seven assistant secretaries and undersecretaries of State, four top members of the Defense Department, and two members of the White House Staff, with Republicans and Democrats liberally mixed.

As far as Congress is concerned, the relationship between the corporate sector and political power is less straightforward. The fact, however, that the majority of congressmen are lawyers provides one mechanism for strong but legal corporate influence over Congress. This situation has been pointed up by veteran Washington reporters Drew Pearson and Jack Anderson, who note that "The back door to many a Congressman's office can be reached through his law practice."

Pearson and Anderson studied fifty typical law firms with partners serving in Congress, and found that they had a "remarkable similarity of clients." Forty of the firms represented banks, thirty-one worked for insurance companies, eleven served gas and oil corporations, and ten represented real estate firms. Interestingly, some of the biggest corporations in the United States, headquartered in the major cities, were served by congressmen's law firms in such booming metropolises as Nicholasville, Kentucky and Pascagoula, Mississippi; these included General Motors, Ford, Standard Oil of New Jersey, Gulf Oil, Sinclair Refining, Aluminum Company of America, Baltimore and Ohio Railroad, Western Union, International Harvester, Seagram Distillers, Coca Cola, and Equitable Life. That many major corporations were serviced by a law firm in Peoria, Illinois, is understandable given the fact that one of its associates was none other than the late Senate Republican leader Everett Dirksen. Pearson and Anderson also made a study of the legislative records of these congressmen lawyers, and found, not surprisingly, that "They have promoted legislation that would benefit banks, utilities, airlines, railroads, oil companies, insurance firms and other corporations that have retained their law firms."

The corporate sector has other levers of influence over both lawyer and nonlawyer congressmen. One extremely important area of influence is contributions. The cost of obtaining a seat in either the House of Representatives or the Senate is rising every year, and is in the tens of thousands of dollars for House seats and in the millions for hotly contested Senate seats. Here again, corporations have an enormous advantage in that their officers and big stockholders are major contributors. While data on this touchy subject are extremely fragmentary, one interesting observation can be drawn from the previously cited study showing that corporate executives contributed almost 20 percent of all major gifts to interstate campaign committees in 1956. Namely, the major corporate donor groups were virtually identical with those extensively hiring congressman lawyers: banking, brokerage, industry, oil, mining, utilities, transport, real estate, and insurance.

Just how crucial these corporate contributions are for reaching the higher levels of government has been indicated by Representative Charles E. Bennett of Florida, a conservative congressman with a unique set of ethics that will not allow him to accept a campaign contribution of more than $200. Bennett was interested in running for the Senate seat being vacated in 1970 by Senator Holland, but found it completely impossible to raise the necessary money:

One of the bigger money raisers in the state said to me, "Charlie, it is not possible to raise a million dollars in Florida *for you.*" I said, "What do you mean, for me?" He said, "Because you would not allow it to be raised in the way it is being raised." I asked, "How is it being raised?" He said, "Money is raised by the process of allowing people in large corporations that have expense accounts to give cash to the candidate and charge it to their expense accounts." Of course this is doubly illegal. In the first place, the corporation is not entitled to give a contribution to a campaign, and secondly, it is undoubtedly reported to the I.R.S. as an expense. This man asked me, "You would not want money raised that way, would you?" I said, "I would not." He said, "Well, that's where the bulk of the money comes from, so forget it." So I forgot it.

An extreme example of how far corporations can go in generating contributions for their favorite sons is detailed by Pearson and Anderson. Senator Robertson, Democrat of Virginia, pushed a bill through Congress in 1965 that legalized six bank mergers that had previously been blocked by the Justice Department as obvious violations of antitrust law. In 1966 Robertson was facing an extremely tough primary campaign, so Manufacturers Hanover Trust Company, one of the six banks aided by Robertson's bill, sent out letters to its 44,000 stockholders who lived all over the country stating, "We believe that Senator Robertson, Senate Office Building, Washington, D.C., would like to know you appreciated his attitude and efforts." Another letter on behalf of Robertson was sent out by the president of a bank in Virginia to all other Virginia bank presidents reminding them that "Senator Robertson has supported us in all banking legislation," and urging them to pressure their employees to make contributions to the Robertson campaign and to vote for him. In this case the corporate pressure was so raw—a director of one Virginia bank even resigned, stating that the "arm-twisting" was too much for him—that Robertson lost the election. But, this was an unusual ending attributable largely to the fact that the blatancy of the corruption generated a great deal of publicity.

There are other less obvious levers of corporate influence over congressmen. For example, defense contractors can open or close plants in a congressman's district, or can offer him free time on the radio and television stations they own or control. This control of radio and television stations has become increasingly important now that RCA, Westinghouse, General Electric, General Tire and Rubber, Avco, and Kaiser, among others, have moved heavily into this area.

Lest one mistakenly think that corporate influence affects only conservative congressmen, listen to this Pearson-Anderson report on a moderate senator:

One of the Senate's most conscientious members—J. William Fulbright, D-Ark.—votes down the line for the oil and gas interests. Talking privately to friends, he once explained apologetically that he could not be re-elected in Arkansas if he bumped his head against the powerful oil bloc.

Epstein notes that "Senators Mike Mansfield of Montana and John O. Pastore of Rhode Island, both having reputations as liberal Democrats, are also well known respectively for their representation of Montana copper interests and of Rhode Island textile manufacturers." Or how else can one explain Senator Hubert Humphrey's continued tolerance of discredited lobbyist Julius Klein, other than as Pearson and Anderson state "A politician without personal wealth does not dismiss a campaign contributor too cavalierly."

Finally, an important source of corporate influence on congressmen arises because many congressmen have a major personal financial stake in the corporate society. The majority of congressmen started out in the lower or middle classes, and while climbing the political ladder have reached the top 1 percent income group. Close to one third of all U.S. senators, for example, are known to be definitely or probably millionaires.

Few are as blatant about their use of political power to increase their own wealth as the late multimillionaire oil senator, Robert Kerr of Oklahoma (founder of the Kerr-McGee Oil Company, one of *Fortune*'s top "500"). Pearson and Anderson report that:

His friend Bobby Baker once recalled, "Bob Kerr used to say that he was opposed to all monopolies unless he had a piece of them." And Kerr himself boasted with a chuckle, "Hell, I'm in everything."

On another occasion Kerr said, "I represent the financial institutions of Oklahoma, and I am interested in them, and they know that, and this is the reason they elect me."

Oil wealth apparently is conducive to such disarming candor, as evidenced by the statements of Senator Russell Long, chairman of the Senate Finance Committee, which has for decades zealously defended the oil depletion allowance. Between 1964 and 1969 Long received about $1.2 million from oil and gas production, of which over $300,000 was tax free thanks to this particular tax loophole. Acknowledging that he is widely known as "the darling of the oil industry," Senator Long sees no conflict of interests but only "an identity of interests."

Congressional involvement in the corporate economy for personal gain is a widespread phenomenon. For example, congressmen have become very active in the savings and loan industry, which has benefited greatly from special legislation. Twenty-six members of the 90th Congress were found to have extensive holdings in savings and loan companies. Even more, congressmen are heavily involved with commercial banks, with records of the Federal Reserve (which show only the top twenty stockholders of each national bank) listing dozens of congressmen and their relatives. There were 97 bankers in the House of Representatives, of which a dozen served on the House Banking Committee. (What the situation is in the Senate is not known because that body has successfully blocked all attempts to force revelation of its members' business ties.) It is no wonder that banking legislation is a great interest of many congressmen.

That this interest is far from academic is dramatized

by the case of Congressman John W. Byrnes of Wisconsin, the ranking Republican on the House Ways and Means Committee, which originates all tax legislation. In 1960 Byrnes used his power to pressure the Internal Revenue Service for a special tax ruling favoring the Mortgage Guaranty Insurance Company of Milwaukee. The ruling helped propel the stock of the company to a tenfold increase, which was a great benefit not only to one of its principal stockholders, Bobby Baker, but also to other congressmen and to Byrnes himself. Byrnes saw no ethical problem here, insisting that he had done nothing that "any other Congressman would not do for a constituent or a business in his state that had a problem," ignoring the fact that Milwaukee was not in his congressional district. Unlike that of Senator Robertson, Byrnes's case did not draw a great deal of public attention and he is still in office. Although at that time there was no "House Ethics Committee," it is unlikely that even today Byrnes would have any problem on this score, given the fact that seven of the twelve members of the Ethics Committee own stock in financial institutions and that four of them are directors.

Another area of great personal congressional involvement for profit is ownership of radio or television stations, an industry in which government licenses to operate are highly valuable. In 1963 no less than thirty-three congressmen, or their relatives, had radio or television interests.

From the foregoing it should be clear that many congressmen are closely linked, both economically and ideologically, to the business community. However, some of this linkage is to local business interests as opposed to the national corporate community; this includes not only local banking and radio and television, but the large plantation interests of numerous southern senators. In addition, since congressmen, particularly in major urban areas, must sometimes be responsive to popular pressures there can be no simple mechanism of corporate control of the Congress. In practice, Congress tends to serve the purposes of particular sections of the corporate economy by "logrolling," in which congressmen representing different business interests swap votes. By the same device Congress serves the purposes of the corporate economy as a whole primarily by acting as a block to any radical change in the status quo. In this connection it is interesting to note that a mid-1968 survey of corporate public activities showed that more than 85 percent of corporate communications to public officials was in *opposition* to proposed legislation.

A crucial institutional barrier to change is provided by the "Congressional Establishment," brilliantly described by former U.S. Senator Joseph Clark in his *Congress: The Sapless Branch.* After noting that "Our forms of government are heavily weighted against any kind of action, and especially any that might alter significantly the status quo" (and pointing out that this was the aim of our Founding Fathers), Clark identifies the congressional Establishment as the Democratic chairmen and the ranking Republican members of important legislative committees. Most of these men are elderly, from the South or rural areas, and share the following "ideals":

The bonds which hold the Congressional Establishment together are: white supremacy; a stronger devotion to property than to human rights; support of the military establishment; belligerence in foreign affairs; and a determination to prevent Congressional reform.

Thus, one basis of the corporate sector's continuing influence over Congress is its general mutuality of interests with these conservative southern and rural legislators, who through the seniority system have become the congressional Establishment.

Despite many years of verbal assault on the congressional Establishment by liberals like Senator Clark, effective congressional reform is as remote as ever. The existence of the congressional Establishment serves as a convenient scapegoat for the majority of congressmen from the major urban areas to justify congressional inaction to their constituents. The lack of real will for congressional reform is shown by the deceptive voting pattern on measures in favor of it. In one session of Congress the House of Representatives will approve reform, but the Senate will do nothing. In the next session the Senate passes the reform legislation but the House does nothing. Since a bill must be passed by both branches of Congress in the same session to become law, congressional reform is never passed, but anyone in the House or Senate can safely be on record as voting in favor of it! Such a strategy is worthy of the best legal minds in the sick society.

Finally, we may briefly examine the relationship between the corporate community and the other two major branches of the federal government, the judiciary and the regulatory agencies.

While there is little data available on the judiciary, some conclusions flow from the logic of the situation. Since the federal judiciary is appointed by the president, insofar as the corporate community controls the presidency, it has influence over the type of men to be appointed to the bench. In addition, the Committee of the Federal Judiciary of the American Bar Association has had an informal veto power over judicial appointments; this arrangement has been made more explicit following the row over Nixon's abortive Supreme Court appointments. The members of this committee tend to be highly successful lawyers practicing in large law firms in major cities—whose practice is heavily for corporate clients. While relationships between the corporate community and the judiciary would be a fertile area for research, in my opinion existing knowledge supports the view of sociologist G. William Domhoff in *Who Rules America?*. After reviewing the evidence Domhoff concludes: "The appointive power of the President, in conjunction with the ABA committee, gives members of the power elite control over the socioeconomic and intellectual character of the federal judiciary."

While one school of thought holds that the regulatory agencies were originally established to help the corporation, others argue that there is a pattern of their metamorphosis from regulators to protectors and apologists for the industry. In fact, some students of the subject have divided the life cycle of a regulatory agency into four periods. In gestation and youth there is great public enthusiasm for regulation and strong efforts by the regulatory agency. In maturity the process of devitalization sets in, and in old age there is debility and decline. This is marked, in Epstein's words, by "gradual identification between the administrators and their clientele, consultation with this clientele prior to appointment of high-level administrative officials, service by business executives in tours of duty as regulators, and cooperation between the agency and its clients in securing legislation appropriations for the agency's work."

Lee Loevinger, chief of the Justice Department's Antitrust Division in the early 1960s, explains how the process takes place:

Unfortunately, the history of every regulatory agency in the government is that it comes to represent the industry or groups it's supposed to control. All of these agencies were fine when they were first set up, but before long they became infiltrated by the regulatees and are now more or less run by and for them. It's not a question of venality, either. More, the agency people consort with this or that representative of some special-interest group, and finally they all come to think alike. Every company that's concerned about government control and is big enough to manage it hires a man—or maybe four or five men—at anywhere from thirty to seventy thousand dollars a year to find out what we're up to. And, by God, they find out! They wine and dine the agency people and get to be great friends with them. Like a lot of people without much money, some bureaucrats are impressed by being around big shots and by the big life. Sooner or later, all of these agencies end up with constituents. And they represent them damned well, too.

The most prominent of the regulatory agencies that experts characterize as having "client control" are the Federal Power Commission, the Federal Communications Commission, the Food and Drug Administration, the Interstate Commerce Commission, and the Civil Aeronautics Board (CAB). There is general agreement that the last two agencies were born in order to protect the regulated industry, and in the case of the CAB to promote it.

As for the enormous array of over fifty thousand state and local governments, it seems likely that the national corporate community would have far less direct influence and/or control over these institutions than it does over Congress. As one study of a small town notes, local government is the stronghold of smaller businessmen: "Since 1939 retail trade, insurance, and real estate have been the predominant occupations of both elected and appointed officials." There is little specific data on the real locus of power for the vast number of local governments in the United States, and much of it is open to conflicting interpretation. Nevertheless, the following analysis by Richard Holton, a business school dean formerly active in government, is a good summary of what is generally know as regards the corporate situation:

The major corporation is not so deeply involved at the level of state and local government as at the federal level. There are exceptions, of course: The large public utility, regulated by the state, is interested in state legislation affecting utility rates; the major insurance company watches the state legislatures' debates about insurance rates; the nationally known manufacturer planning a new plant deals with local officials about zoning regulations; and in some states a handful of corporations are so dominant that they, perforce, play an influential role in the state capital. But the large corporation is primarily concerned with the policies of the federal government. Its influence at the state and local level is typically less significant. Although the top executive in the company may exhort the troops to become involved in politics, the rising young executive in the company is not likely to wield much power at the state and local level. He is struggling up the corporate ladder and has limited time for politics. More important, he is transferred so often that he cannot build a solid political base from which to be effective. Thus, business influence on state and local governments may be primarily the influence of the owners of the medium-sized and small firms, while the business influence on the federal government may be much more heavily weighted toward the views of the major corporations.

Finally, this chapter would not be complete without an examination of the increasingly important nonprofit institutions in the United States. The most important of these are the universities and the foundations. Their rapid growth in recent years has led to great concern about them as rising power centers; this is sometimes linked to a purported decline of corporate power. Thus, as noted, Galbraith already sees the shift of power to the "technocracy," which is rooted in the university. Sociologist Daniel Bell is more cautious: "Perhaps it is not too much to say that if the business firm was the key institution of the past hundred years, because of its role in organizing production for the mass creation of products, the university will become the central institution of the next hundred years because of its role as the new source of innovation and knowledge."

Be that as it may, it is useful to put the present relative power positions of these nonprofit institutions into realistic perspective. The "University Industry" consists of about 2,000 institutions with annual revenues of $10 billion. While there is no definitive data on tax exempt foundations, it has been estimated that they number perhaps as many as 100,000; the 550 largest ones, which undoubtably control the bulk of the foundations' economic resources, had an income of about $1 billion in 1960 and assets of about $10 billion. Allowing for inflation and the growth of foundation assets, it may reasonably be estimated that today all tax exempt foundations have assets on the order of $20 billion and incomes of $2 billion.

From these figures it is clear that the nonprofit institutions are economic pygmies as compared to the major corporations. American Telephone & Telegraph (AT&T) alone has assets of close to $40 billion, revenues of $15 billion, and after-tax profits of $2 billion. Yet, one rarely hears reference to AT&T as a major power institution. The hundred largest U.S. manufacturing companies have close to $200 billion in assets, revenues on the same order of magnitude, and after-tax income of close to $20 billion annually.

The reason for stressing these relative economic magnitudes is simple. Power in our society is fundamentally determined by an institution's ability to harness material and human resources toward achieving its goals. Clearly then, the institutions that have the greatest stock of assets as well as the greatest flows of income normally have the most control over resources, and hence the greatest power. This is not to say that the nonprofit institutions have no independent power. For one thing, there are important cases where, for estate tax purposes, control blocs of major corporations have been lodged in foundations, e.g., Ford Motor, A & P, Eli Lilly, Kellogg Company, Duke Power, and S.S. Kresge. Nevertheless, corporations generally wield a great deal of power over both foundations and universities because the corporations are major financial contributors. This is true despite the fact that business can contribute on a tax deductible basis up to 5 percent of its gross income, yet now donates less than 1 percent. Such is the enormous horn of corporate plenty from which little rivulets trickle.

Another source of corporate control that goes hand in hand with its financial donor powers is corporate domination of the board of trustees of nonprofit institutions. Columbia University's twenty-two trustees include the president or chairman of the board of United Artists, CBS, *The New York Times,* Consolidated Edison, and Uris Building Corporation. Among them the twenty-two trustees hold over forty directorships in major corporations such as Bankers Trust, Lockheed Aircraft, Allied Chemical, Mobil Oil, IBM, Consolidated Edison, Union Pacific Railroad, American Electric Power, Standard Oil of New Jersey, AT&T, Chase Manhattan Bank, General Foods, International Paper, Whirlpool, Time, General Dynamics, and First National City Bank. At Harvard the situation is similar. There, the seven men who run the Harvard Corporation hold the chairmanship of Mobil Oil, as well as almost twenty directorships, including those of Metropolitan Life Insurance, First National Bank of Maryland, American Airlines, Amerada Petroleum, Crowell Collier and Macmillan, Middle South Utilities, John Hancock Insurance, and Commonwealth Oil Refining.

It is true that the nonprofit organization-corporate relationship is a two-way street. Thus, one-fourth of *Fortune*'s top 200 industrial corporations have university officials sitting on their boards of directors. The critical point, however, is that while the corporation clearly benefits from the advice and consulting services of university officials, the corporation itself is the wellspring of power. The corporation hires the university officials as directors and provides the nonprofit organization with the basic sources of their funds. In turn, the foundations and universities provide skilled people for the corporation (as well as for government, and increasingly serve as a temporary resting place for ex-government officials).

It is necessary to emphasize that while there is a great deal of interlock and flow of personnel between the corporations, the political institutions, and the nonprofit organizations, the corporations as controllers of the bulk of the economic resources of the country are the power base from which the others sprout. This real power relationship is often obscured because university intellectuals —the people who write most frequently about these relationships—tend to overestimate their own powers, while underestimating corporate powers. This is a mistake that the corporations are quite happy to let stand uncorrected. (Unlike the suggestion of the advertising campaign for a major airline, the corporations generally follow the wise precept that "when you've got it, don't flaunt it" if you want to hold on to it.) A perceptive journalist, James Ridgeway, has aptly summarized the real state of the relationships between the universities, government, and business, as well as the delusions of scholars as to which party truly holds the reins of power:

The theory is that the activities of the corporations can be planned and set in motion by scholars who scheme together at their innards. Other scholars within the government make sure the goals of production are worthy, and to control the activity of the corporations, they ring changes through the economic machinery, as, for example, in the late Senator Robert Kennedy's slum rehabilitation plan. Its central feature is to bring outside economic support into the ghetto and yet promote the illusion of black control. *In fact, the control remains with the large corporations,* which in return for widening their power base are slightly more beneficent, hiring some blacks but passing on the cost of their involvement to the consumers through higher prices.

So the scholars dash back and forth, building the new economic and political machinery. They see themselves as renaissance men, the proprietors of the new factories.

This chapter has attempted to make a *prima facie* case for the existence of corporate control over the American political structure by examining structural relationships. One case study in how these structural relationships actually function concerns the success of the major corporations and their wealthy stockholders in beating down the threat of the new conglomerate take-overs.

In the frenzied speculative heyday of the conglomerates which climaxed in 1968, even successful companies began to fear a take-over; there was talk that even General Motors and United States Steel might not be immune from acquisition. Underlying this struggle between established companies and the new conglomerates was a fight between two wings of American capital: large established wealth, such as that represented by the Rockefellers, Morgans, DuPonts, Fords, and other leading families of the tiny economic elite, and smaller but growing "upstart" wealth. Much of the latter was unacceptable to the Establishment for social reasons. For one thing, a number of the new conglomerates are run by Jews, e.g., Charles Bludhorn of Gulf and Western Industries, the Tisch brothers of Loew's, Ben Heineman of Northwest Industries, Meshulam Riklis of the McCrory-Glen Alden-Rapid American Industries complex, and Saul Steinberg of Leasco Data Processing. Others were headed by *nouveaux riches* like Jimmy Ling of the billion dollar Ling-Temco-Vought, Inc., who was originally a Texas poor boy. While the clash of social values embodied in the conglomerate-Establishment corporate struggle is dramatic, it should not obscure the basic fact that the real anger of the old wealth came from the threat to its economic interests; after all, another Texas poor boy named Lyndon Johnson proved perfectly acceptable to the corporate Establishment.

This economic threat arose partly because of the acquisition techniques developed successfully by the conglomerates. Typically, a conglomerate would offer fifty dollars worth of its stock or bonds to the shareholders of an Establishment company selling at thirty dollars per share. This would induce small stockholders to tender their stock to the conglomerate since they could then sell their relatively small quantities of the new stock at a quick profit. However, such a road is not easily open to the very large stockholders. If they tried to sell their large blocks of new stock this could depress its price greatly. Moreover, big, established wealth normally has owned its stock for a long time and would incur serious tax disadvantages selling out. This strengthened its basic unwillingness to place control of its companies in the hands of the conglomerate operators.

As a result, Establishment wealth fought back using both its political and economic power. The *Wall Street Journal* reported in early 1969 that pressures were mounting on both Democrats and Republicans in Congress to move against the conglomerates, with the heaviest pressure "coming from older companies that are resisting take-over bids." At that time a bill was introduced into Congress (to be retroactive to the date of introduction), and later approved, which specified tax penalties for bonds issued for the purpose of take-overs. Additionally, a whole panoply of government investigators, including the Federal Trade Commission, the Securities and Exchange Commission, and House and Senate committees began investigations into the conglomerates. Finally, the Justice Department's Antitrust Division warned that it would take action against conglomerate mergers.

The use or misuse of antitrust policy dramatically illustrates how big corporations wield mighty political power and control government policy that crucially affects them. Both political parties bend over backward to avoid use of the antitrust laws to curtail the power of Establishment corporations. Thus, Richard Barber (former counsel to the Senate Subcommittee on Anti-trust) states that President Johnson's response to his own task force's report recommending dismembering such giant corporations as GM, IBM, and U.S. Steel was not only to suppress it, but to deny that the report even existed. The new Nixon administration, upon receiving its own secret task force recommendations of "a policy of strict and unremitting scrutiny of the highly oligopolistic [i.e., monopolistic] industries" not only refused to release the report but was unwilling to admit that the task force even existed! As Barber comments on this Alice in Wonderland exhibition, "Both the Democratic and Republican administrations provided explicit evidence of their distaste for proposals that might lead to the substantial deconcentration of American industry," i.e., to the breakup of big, established corporate power.

On the other hand, the new Nixon administration moved with alacrity to interpret antitrust law, for the first time, against conglomerate mergers. Can cautious corporate lawyer Nixon's haste to develop novel legal doctrines (in the words of his Assistant Attorney General, "The matter of [conglomerate mergers] is too pressing to wait [for congressional legislation]") be unrelated to the fact that, as Barber concludes, the new approach's "real impact will be to shield large, well entrenched companies, like Jones and Laughlin and B.F. Goodrich, from takeover by conglomerate outsiders like LTV and Northwest Industries"? Does it take a complete cynic to see some link between this action and big corporate money swinging back to the Republican party in 1968?

The high watermark of the conglomerate tide was the bold attempt of Saul Steinberg, twenty-nine-year-old president of Leasco Data Processing Equipment Corp., to take over Chemical Bank. Leasco was not big enough to be in *Fortune*'s top five hundred industrial companies, while Chemical was the country's sixth largest bank with assets of almost $10 billion. Successful efforts were made, involving what *The New York Times* reported as "fantastic" pressure by other banks as well as by Leasco's corporate customers, to force Steinberg to abandon his take-over plans. Political pressure was exerted by New York's Governor Nelson Rockefeller, who requested immediate legislation to protect banks in New York State from take-overs, and by the Nixon administration's introduction of a comparable bill in Congress covering national banks. Because of the major stakes involved for the Establishment, the realities of big capital control of major U.S. corporations and the political apparatus, which are normally subsurface, emerged into the open. *Business Week* quoted Steinberg as lamenting: "I always knew there was an Establishment, I just used to think I was part of it," and pointed out the correct moral:

Leasco's abortive play last February for giant Chemical Bank of New York threw Steinberg against the real establishment of big, conservative money—a confrontation so jarring that Wall Street still clucks about it. In the end, says a Wall Street friend, "Saul found out there really is a back room where the big boys sit and smoke their long cigars."

The conclusions of this chapter may be seen as a series of hypotheses about the anatomical structure of the sick society. The corporate economy more or less directly controls the federal executive government. It has strong influence on the federal congressional, judicial, and regulatory apparatus and major nonprofit institutions. It has least influence over the various state and local governments. In the next part we shall test these hypotheses by examining over a wide range the actual operative relationships between the corporate economy and the various ills of the sick society.

CHRONIC ILLNESSES

3

UNITED STATES
OVERSEAS INVOLVEMENT

The Vietnam War is acknowledged to be a core problem among all strata of the sick society. It is increasingly obvious even to diehard reactionaries that the Vietnam War has heightened racial tensions and contributes tremendously to the sense of alienation among youth and intellectuals. For these reasons, not to mention, of course, the tremendous economic cost of the war, there is now a consensus that it must be ended soon.

At the same time, however, there is majority agreement that our involvement in the Vietnam War is essentially a tragic "historical accident." In the words of liberal spokesman Arthur Schlesinger, Jr.:

We have achieved this entanglement, not after due and deliberate consideration, but through a series of small decisions. . . . Each step in the deepening of the American commitment was reasonably regarded at the time as the last that would be necessary; yet, in retrospect, each step led only to the next, until we find ourselves entrapped today in that nightmare of American strategists, a land war in Asia—a war which no President, including President Johnson, desired or intended. The Vietnam story is a tragedy without villains.

The logical corollary of this "accident" theory is that once the Vietnam War is ended, U.S. foreign policy will largely return to its normal munificent past of friendly and peaceful relationships with the rest of the world (perhaps excluding the present communist countries, particularly China).

My aim in this chapter is to refute this theory by showing that our involvement in Vietnam as well as in other parts of the world is no accident. Rather, it is part of a pattern of widespread foreign involvement stemming basically from U.S. economic expansionism. Moreover, such involvement and expansionism is itself a logical and necessary outgrowth of the corporate society.

Before embarking upon a detailed analysis of the relationship between the corporate economy and U.S. foreign policy it will be useful to compare my thesis with the more general liberal analyses of foreign policy. One of the most sophisticated of these is that of Ronald Steel in his recent book *Pax Americana*. Steel concedes that the United States has built up a world empire, but sees this as the accidental by-product of a moral crusade:

> . . . the American empire came into being by accident and has been maintained from a sense of benevolence. Nobody planned our empire. In fact, nobody even wanted it. . . .
>
> Unlike Rome, we have not exploited our empire. On the contrary, our empire has exploited us, making enormous drains on our resources and our energies. . . .
>
> . . . we have never conceived of it as an empire. Rather, we

saw it as a means of containing communism, and thereby permitting other nations to enjoy the benefits of freedom, democracy, and self-determination.

Steel recognizes that our "moral crusade" in defense of freedom did not prevent us from strongly supporting dozens of right-wing dictatorships. He concludes that the fundamental error in U.S. foreign policy was to become overextended because of a "confusion" of anticommunism with "national interest":

Yugoslavia is communist; so are Albania and North Korea. What benefit does the Soviet Union get out of that? Or China, for that matter? Nicaragua is anti-communist; so are Taiwan and South Korea. What good does that do us? As far as the national interest is concerned, it makes little difference what kind of ideology a government professes, so long as it does not follow policies which are hostile or dangerous.

The trouble with this analysis is that it fails to recognize the primacy of American economic interests, rather than military security, in determining U.S. foreign policy. This is *not* to say that economic interests are always the sole or overriding determinant of American foreign policy decisions. For one thing, as I have argued earlier, the country's political leaders are not simply puppets of the major corporations. These leaders have their own interests and goals which on occasion may differ from those of the corporations; moreover, they may sometimes have a different view of what is best for the corporate community in the long run, particularly when the latter is divided as to strategy. I do claim, however, that the power of the corporate community to influence foreign policy decision makers and decisions, along with the general harmony of interest among economic, military, and political expansionists, is sufficient to make economic interests the propelling force of U.S. foreign policy.

Once granted that economic interests play the major role in foreign policy, then it makes a great deal of difference whether a country is communist and/or socialist, or capitalist, even if the country is totally incapable of threatening us militarily. Each country that shifts from the capitalist to the socialist world is a country where the United States loses valuable existing investments as well as potential outlets for profitable future investment (and possibly trade). In the words of the former U.S. ambassador to the Soviet Union, "Every time the Soviet Union extends its power over another area or state the United States and Great Britain lose another normal market." Thus, one "good" that Taiwan does us is that under that dictatorship U.S. investment has grown from virtually nothing in 1950 to many millions of dollars today, with much more planned for the future. One harm that Cuba does us is that a United States investment in 1960 of $1 billion was suddenly made worthless.

Moreover, it is in the economic area that the "domino theory," which Mr. Steel views as a subordinate fallacy underlying U.S. foreign policy, has real validity. A successful economy in Taiwan does not give greater "military protection" to Southeast Asia, but may buttress capitalist forces in the area. More significantly, a successful Cuban socialist economy, by providing an attractive alternative road to economic development, poses a grave long-run threat to U.S. economic interests in all of the stagnating underdeveloped world.

Steel's analysis at the abstract level of the (undefined) "national interest" also overlooks the fundamental fact that in the sick society the "national interest" is not merely some arithmetic sum of individual citizens' interests. In determining foreign policy some are more equal than others. How could it be otherwise in our society when the major international corporations, which wield great political power at home, have such enormous and farflung overseas interests that they are almost automatically deeply concerned with and involved in American foreign policy? Or when American businessmen abroad are enlisted as sources of intelligence for the State Department and Central Intelligence Agency alike?

To take the outstanding example, Standard Oil of New Jersey has close to $10 billion of its capital at work in foreign operations that encompass most of the noncommunist world. In order to operate this vast empire it has three times as many overseas employees as the State Department. Jersey's superior intelligence gathering reputation was illuminated in a novel by a former World War II intelligence officer. One of his characters, a church official, ranks the Vatican's intelligence service as second only to Standard Oil, with both far ahead of the State Department. This intelligence is a vital element in shaping Jersey's own foreign policy; more important, the two-way flow of personnel—as well as information—between Jersey (and the oil industry in general) and the government's foreign policy apparatus assures Jersey of a sympathetic ear for its position. The fact that a relatively small number of international corporations have anywhere near Jersey's influence, suggests that in analyzing major foreign policy decisions it is sometimes necessary not only to look beyond the "national interest" but also to uncover the specific corporate interests involved as well as the overall interest of the corporate community.

It is undoubtedly true that the American empire is not

the result of a master plan to conquer the world. This does not mean, however, that this empire was created "accidentally." This empire basically has grown as the corporate society has pushed outward. This growth in turn reflects the fact that each major corporation in the sick society is a power center that seeks to develop monopolistic enclaves of empire for itself, in competition with other corporations. There is thus no coordinated grand design to lay siege to one country or another. Nevertheless, while it may be an accident of nature that Saudi Arabia has vast oil reserves or Chile has copper or Guatemala has bananas or Liberia has rubber, it is no accident that the major U.S. corporations which carve out their own empires—the four-company consortium in Saudi Arabia, Anaconda and Kennecott in Chile, United Fruit in Guatemala, Firestone in Liberia—then use all of their vast resources to influence U.S. foreign policy to protect them. Moreover, as will be shown later, there are important cases where the U.S. government itself provided the means for individual corporations to add to the empire.

This is not to deny that from the corporate viewpoint, *in retrospect,* the Vietnam War was a ghastly error. After all, corporate leaders and the corporate mentality, both of which flood Washington, are far from infallible. In particular, there is a serious flaw in the corporate type of thinking that emphasizes profit maximization and "discounting the future." This approach tends toward narrow policies stressing immediacy and involves systematic underestimation of subtle distinctions and long-run effects. In addition the overall success of U.S. foreign policy in the last two decades has created that "fatal arrogance of power" which leads to underestimating one's antagonists.

Whatever lessons may be learned from the Vietnam

debacle are likely to be strictly tactical, because the drive for overseas economic expansion is fundamental to U.S. foreign policy. This is because such expansion is, and will continue to be, a necessity for the corporate economy. To support this argument, in the remainder of this chapter I shall attempt to document three main ideas:

1. that the economy in general and the corporate Establishment in particular has a major and growing stake in overseas economic relations;

2. that the foreign policy officials of the federal government are closely tied to the corporate Establishment;

3. that U.S. foreign policy has largely been an instrument for promoting these corporate economic interests.

To begin with, it has traditionally been argued that the United States, alone among the developed countries of the non-communist world, is virtually free from dependence upon foreign economic relations. The standard method of "proving" this has been to point to the fact that United States exports as a percentage of the gross national product (GNP, or the value of all goods and services produced) are relatively low; the figure is about 5 percent, compared to about 20 percent for Great Britain, West Germany, and Canada, 15 percent for France, and 10 percent for Japan. While it is conceded that the United States is the world's leading foreign investor, the fact that annual U.S. foreign investment is about one-seventh of domestic U.S. investment is taken to "prove" its relative unimportance to our economy.

The fact is, however, as has been brilliantly shown by economist Harry Magdoff in his book, *The Age of Imperialism,* these ratios are seriously misleading. For one thing, included in the GNP are the value of a great many kinds of services, e.g., the activities of bankers, traders, real estate brokers, etc., which are dependent upon the level of activity in the goods production sector. For this reason, in assessing the economic importance of exports, the U.S. Department of Commerce compares them not with the GNP, but with the total domestic production of "moveable goods," i.e., sales of agricultural products, minerals, manufactures, and freight receipts. Since these moveable goods account for about one-half of the GNP, it is clear that comparing exports with them alone would double the apparent relative significance of exports. Moreover, it is the production of goods, rather than services, which is primarily the domain of the leading corporations.

Far more important, however, is that the export/GNP analysis ignores the enormous American stake in foreign investment. As every businessman knows, there are two ways to penetrate a foreign market: either export from home or build a factory abroad. For a variety of reasons, including the tariff barriers surrounding the European Common Market, increasingly in recent years U.S. firms have found the most profitable way is through overseas investment rather than export. As a result, it has been estimated by the authoritative National Industrial Conference Board that while U.S. exports were only $25 billion in 1964, the value of overseas output resulting from U.S. foreign investment was $143 billion, or almost six times as much as the exports. While the $168 billion of exports plus overseas output cannot be directly compared to the $280 billion of domestic goods output, using these data, Magdoff has made some estimates that give a true indication of the enormous American stake in overseas markets: "We arrive at a conservative estimate that *the size of the foreign market (for domestic and United States-owned foreign firms) is equal to approximately two-fifths the domestic output of farms, factories, and mines.*"

Another factor that makes the U.S. foreign stake even greater than might appear otherwise is that foreign investment is generally more profitable than domestic investment. In 1969, according to Department of Commerce figures, earnings on all U.S. private foreign investments amounted to one-fourth of the after tax profits of all U.S. nonfinancial corporations.

It should also be noted that at any point in time exports may have a disproportionate effect on corporate profits. This is due to the existence in most large corporations of high fixed costs; additional sales that allow the spreading of these fixed costs over a larger volume increase unit profits and thus have a multiplier effect on total profits.

For critical sectors of the economy, foreign involvement is even more crucial than might be expected from the overall economic data. One reason is that, as I shall attempt to document later, military expenditures are a concomitant of maintaining and increasing our foreign investment and markets. In turn, military expenditures and exports have an exceptionally large impact on the capital goods industry, which historically has been the crucial transmission mechanism for boom and bust in the U.S. economy. Thus, while military expenditures plus exports amount to only 15 percent of the GNP, together they account for a share of the total output of most capital goods firms which ranges between 20 and 90 percent. When one further takes into account the previously discussed leverage effect of extra sales on profits, it is clear that for many capital goods corporations, most, if not all, of their profits are dependent upon exports and military expenditures.

Foreign involvement is also extremely important to the major corporations in terms of control of "strategic" raw materials. For them, "strategic" materials may be defined as those enabling them to earn monopolistic profits. In an economic system like ours, the "tail wags the dog": it is the activity at the margin that controls prices, profits, and the stability of the entire economy. Thus, an extra 5 percent supply of oil or bauxite or copper thrown on the market can drive down prices by several times that amount, and depress profits by an even greater factor. The need for insuring that no such "disruptive" independent sources of supply become available gives an added impetus to the major corporations to snatch control of all known possible supply sources.

Happily for the major internationally oriented corporations, their strategic interests can often be equated with U.S. defense needs. Thus, Clarence Randall, former president of Inland Steel Company, rhapsodizes about the fortuitous location of much of the world's uranium deposits in the then Belgian Congo, and, by implication, urges the acquisition of control over others:

What a break it was for us that the mother country was on our side! And who can possibly foresee today which of the vast unexplored areas of the world may likewise possess some unique deposit of a rare raw material which in the fullness of time our industry or our defense program may most urgently need?

For over half of the Defense Department's list of sixty-two strategic industrial materials, imports account for 80 to 100 percent of the new supply; for five-sixths of them at least 40 percent of the supply has to be imported. Taking the jet engine as an important and typical example, of six critical materials used in it, for three of them (columbium, chromium, and cobalt) the United States was 100 percent dependent on imports, for one (nickel),

75 percent dependent on imports, and for one (tungsten) 24 percent dependent on imports.

Perhaps even more significant in terms of the influence of the corporate economy upon foreign policy is the fact that U.S. foreign investment is closely concentrated among a small number of extremely large and important corporations. Indicative of the fact that this, too, is a sensitive nerve in the sick society, the latest government data are for 1957. They show that only forty-five firms, each with a direct overseas investment of over $100 million, account for almost three-fifths of all U.S. direct foreign investment. These are the giant oil, chemical, auto, rubber, and electronic firms that dominate the domestic economy as well.

Moreover, this crucial internationally oriented corporate sector is the base of the larger community of bankers and corporate lawyers who dominate U.S. foreign policy. Gabriel Kolko's study of over 200 high level foreign policy decision makers in the 1944-60 period revealed that men with backgrounds in either big business, banking and investment, or corporate law held three-fifths of all the key posts; furthermore, the most active of these men, those holding at least four posts during this period, virtually all came from the largest and most powerful firms in their fields. Thus, the fact that John Foster Dulles's law firm, Sullivan and Cromwell (counselors to companies like Standard Oil of New Jersey), or James Forrestal's investment banking company, Dillon, Read (bankers for many international corporate giants), placed many men in the top foreign policy posts shows that this permeation is not sporadic and coincidental but continuing and intrinsic. In Kolko's words, his study reveals:

. . . that foreign policy decision-makers are in reality a highly mobile sector of the American corporate structure, a group of men who frequently assume and define high level policy tasks in government, rather than routinely administer it, and then return to business. Their firms and connections are large enough to afford them the time to straighten out or formulate government policy while maintaining their vital ties with giant corporate law, banking, or industry.

The question still remains as to whether this corporate sector dominance in terms of foreign policy personnel affects the actual extent and nature of U.S. overseas involvement. It may be argued by some that these policy makers are simply the most capable people who shuck off their corporate connections upon entering government and promote a foreign policy for the "national interest." In this connection, let us briefly recapitulate the conventional wisdom theory of the underlying motives in recent U.S. foreign policy.

This majority view sees post-World War II U.S. foreign policy as essentially a defensive response to the threat of communist (first Soviet and later Chinese) military agression. In this view the main battlefield was originally Western Europe, where in order to stop communism in the late 1940s the United States poured billions of dollars into Europe through the Marshall Plan. While this was successful in stopping the Soviet juggernaut, from 1950 on, beginning with the Korean War, the Maginot line was transplanted to Asia. There, for two decades the United States has spent additional hundreds of billions of dollars plus tens of thousands of its lives to prevent communist aggression and take-over.

Nowhere in this view do American foreign investments or trade or profits play any significant role. The fact that these economic interests have expanded tremendously is seen as unrelated, or as a coincidental by-product of our military efforts plus other "accidental" phenomena, e.g., the postwar weakness of the European powers led to our "inheriting" their economic interests in former colonies. In what follows I propose to challenge this conventional view by examining the circumstances surrounding major U.S. interventions in the postwar period. In particular the focus will be on the extent to which U.S. foreign economic interests have been involved in this intervention.

As background, we need to keep in mind that there is little in the history of the United States of America to suggest any massive or consistent aversion to an economically expansionist foreign policy. On one level, the history of the United States until the Civil War consists of a series of territorial expansions emanating from the small colonies on the eastern seaboard. That the boundaries of the United States do not now extend completely to the Arctic is simply due to the military failure of the attempted 1775-76 annexation of Canada; the southwestern United States is a testimonial to Mexico's lack of similar good fortune.

The prevailing mythology of a normally peaceful America is shattered by Harry Magdoff's calculation: "Adding up the months during which U.S. military forces were engaged in action—starting from the Revolutionary War and including wars against the Indians, punitive expeditions to Latin America and Asia, as well as major wars— we find that the United States was engaged in warlike activity during three-fourths of its history, in 1,782 of the last 2,340 months." During a 1969 Senate debate, Senate Republican leader Everett Dirksen, in defense of his opposition to congressional restraints on presidential action abroad, put into the *Congressional Record* a list of previous U.S. interventions unsanctioned by Congress.

Taking only the section of this fascinating list covering the 1900-40 period, we find that U.S. troops intervened in the following countries: China, twelve times; Honduras, seven times; Panama, six times; Nicaragua, four times; the Dominican Republic, four times; Cuba, three times; Colombia, Haiti, Korea, Turkey, and the Soviet Union, two times each; and Costa Rica, Guatemala, Morocco, and Syria. Furthermore, in half of the cases cited above American property interests are listed as justification for our military intervention.

Economist Eliot Janeway notes, "We have underestimated the economic consequences of our wars . . . the economic role of war has been subordinated instead of acknowledged as the driving force which has again and again paced our historical cycles of expansion. . . ." World War II was certainly no exception to this rule. For one thing, the New Deal had failed to cure the problems of the depression, and only war and war preparations gave jobs to the ten million unemployed in 1939 while carrying the country into a period of prosperity.

At the same time, World War II broke the back of the rival European economic powers, thus allowing American business aggressively to expand not only in Europe but also in her former colonies and spheres of influence. Germany, for example, prior to World War II had amassed an investment of about $1 billion in Latin America, a large sum for that time. This investment was confiscated as a result of the war, as were smaller Japanese and Italian holdings. The big loser, however, was the nominal wartime victor, Great Britain. The latter's investment in Canada dropped from $2.5 billion in 1939 to $1.6 billion in 1947, while her investment in Latin America fell from $4.5 billion in 1939 to $2.6 billion in 1949. Partly because of Britain's need to sell off its overseas investments to purchase U.S. war supplies, during roughly comparable periods American investment rose from $4.2 billion to $5.2 billion in Canada and from $3.7 billion to $5.2 billion in Latin America.

Despite the emergence of the United States from World War II with its economic power at a peak, along with the weakening and/or destruction of its main economic rivals, there were widespread fears about the postwar period. Corporate executives and political leaders worried that without the stimulus of war the economy would sink back into its depression state. The solution seemed to lie in American economic expansion abroad. Thus, in 1944 Assistant Secretary of State Dean Acheson advised a congressional committee studying the possible economic problems of the postwar period, "So far as I know no group which has studied this problem, and there have been many, as you know, has ever believed that our domestic markets could absorb our entire production under our present system." In an unwitting indictment of the sick society, Acheson flatly declared that "you could probably fix it so that everything produced here would be consumed here," but added: "That would completely change our Constitution, our relations to property, human liberty, our very conceptions of law. And nobody contemplates that. Therefore, you find you must look to other markets and those markets are abroad."

As early as December 1940, in a prescient speech before the Investment Bankers Association in New York, Virgil Jordan, president of the prestigious National Industrial Conference Board, stated:

Whatever the outcome of the war, America has embarked on a career of imperialism in world affairs and in every other aspect of her life. . . . At best, England will become a junior partner in a new Anglo-Saxon imperialism, in which the economic resources and the military and naval strength of the United States will be the center of gravity.

Even more significant was the 1946 speech of Leo D. Welch, treasurer of Standard Oil of New Jersey, in which he defined the postwar U.S. foreign policy role as follows:

That responsibility is positive and vigorous leadership in the affairs of the world—political, social, and economic—and it must be fulfilled in the broadest sense of the term. As the largest producer, the largest source of capital, and the biggest contributor to the global mechanism, we must set the pace and assume the responsibility of the majority stockholder in this corporation known as the world. . . . Nor is this for a given term of office. This is a permanent obligation.

That this expansionist attitude would meet a ready reception from U.S. foreign policy could be considered assured. In 1945, John Loftus of the State Department, writing about the relationship between the government and its giant international oil companies, stated:

. . . a review of diplomatic history of the past 35 years will show that petroleum has historically played a larger part in the external relations of the United States than any other commodity.

. . . it seems probable that at least for the first half dozen years after the war the problems will be greater and more difficult than at any time in the past. . . .

. . . this Government must nevertheless recognize and proclaim that international commerce, predicated upon free trade and *private enterprise* (*which is the conceptual core of United States economic foreign policy*), is, in the long run, incompatible with an extensive spread of state ownership and operation of commercial properties.

Another major category of problems concerns the support given by the Department on behalf of the United States Government to American nationals seeking to obtain or to retain rights to engage in petroleum development, transportation, and processing abroad. This is the traditional function of the Department with respect to petroleum.

In 1946 Standard Oil's treasurer, Leo D. Welch, had suggested a crucial way in which the corporate goal of an expansionist foreign policy could be implemented: "As our country has begun to evolve its overall postwar foreign policy, private enterprise must begin to evolve its foreign policy, starting with the most important contribution it can make—'men in government'." That in fact the business community was highly successful in placing its top people in the government after World War II is shown by reporter Howard K. Smith's study of the 125 most important government appointments of President Truman in 1946-47; while one-quarter were military men, one-half were bankers, industrialists, or corporate lawyers. As Smith put it, "The effective locus of government seemed to shift from Washington to some place equidistant between Wall Street and West Point."

The European Cooperation Administration, better known as the Marshall Plan since its conception in June 1947 by General George C. Marshall, was the first major massive U.S. foreign intervention after World War II. During the late 1940s and early 1950s $13 billion of U.S. aid was poured into Western European countries. The Marshall Plan simultaneously served several purposes for the United States. First, it achieved its stated aim of preventing Western European countries from going socialist or communist. The most blatant U.S. intervention apparently came in the Italian election of

1948. A communist-socialist coalition given an "even chance" by Western observers to gain a majority of the votes ended up with only 30 percent. According to Smith, the "most important factor in the turning of the tide was the frank, open entrance of America into the campaign." Among other things, prior to the election, Marshall enunciated the doctrine that "benefits under ERP [the Marshall Plan] will come to an abrupt end in any country that votes Communism into power." As David Horowitz notes, "Given the dollar crisis in Europe, which had hit the Italians particularly hard, this threat alone might have sufficed to swing the elections."

The anticommunist goals of the Marshall Plan, however, had a strong economic base. Will Clayton, head of the large privately owned food processing corporation, Clayton, Anderson, Inc., and Undersecretary of State for Economic Affairs, made this clear in a 1947 speech to the New York Citizens Committee on the Marshall Plan:

> The Marshall Plan is not a relief program; it is a recovery program for Western Europe. Hence, our interests rather than our humanitarian instincts should be mainly considered. . . . [Without this U.S. aid] the Iron Curtain would then move westward at least to the English Channel. Consider what this would mean to us in economic terms alone. A blackout of the European market could compel radical readjustments in our entire economic structure . . . changes which could hardly be made under our democratic free enterprise system.

A second purpose served by the Marshall Plan was to provide immediate markets for American products. This was particularly important because of the fears of a major postwar depression. In fact, many of the products sent to Europe under the Marshall Plan enabled American companies not only to make profitable export sales, but also to maintain high profits at home by reducing supplies available for domestic consumption.

For example, during the first nine months of 1949, 60 to 80 percent of all U.S. exports of corn, copper products, oil seeds, wheat, flour, cotton, tobacco, and peanuts went to the Marshall Plan countries. With regard to peanuts, the chief of food procurement for the U.S. Army Civilian Supply Program in Germany testified that they were so high priced that it was impossible to sell them anywhere else in the world. In fact, he reported his program was forced to buy the peanuts even though they would have preferred to purchase other fats and lards available at more reasonable prices.

Even more significant, between 1948 and 1952 the Marshall Plan financed almost $2 billion worth of European oil imports, most of which were supplied by the five leading U.S. international oil companies. Overcharging by the companies on these shipments was so blatant that the administration ultimately was moved to discontinue such financing. In the interim, however, this Marshall Plan business was a particular bonanza to the international oil companies since it allowed them large-scale outlets for their post-war discoveries of low-cost Middle Eastern crude oil; probably close to 90 percent of the value of the shipments was clear profit.

Finally, the Marshall Plan also served a longer range U.S. policy goal of furthering investment in Europe and European colonies, while at the same time slowing the recovery of European challengers. For example, U.S. oil companies were able to buy out existing refining and marketing facilities in Europe and Japan and erect new ones (some of them covered by investment guarantees under the Marshall Plan); at the same time European rivals such as Royal Dutch Shell were blocked from obtaining the latest American equipment.

With the outbreak of the Korean War in 1950, the focus of American foreign policy began to shift away from Europe to the underdeveloped world. This shift resulted partly because the Korean War itself gave a big boost to the European and Japanese economies, thereby reducing revolutionary pressures from within. Thus, in the course of the 1950s while the U.S. economy grew at a respectable annual rate of 3.2 percent, the comparable growth rates were: West Germany, 7.8 percent, Italy, 5.8 percent, France, 4.6 percent, and Japan, 9.4 percent. The rapid growth of these countries in turn accelerated U.S. interest in the underdeveloped countries, since ever increasing profits could be made from exporting their raw materials to the developed countries.

At the same time, the widespread struggle for political and economic independence in the underdeveloped world caused great ferment in the 1950s. Given the combination of rapidly growing U.S. foreign investment in the underdeveloped world (at least partly because investors were "reassured" by U.S. intervention in Korea), the rise of communist China, and the post-Stalin era Soviet wooing of these countries, it was almost inevitable that the "third world" would become the focal point of U.S. foreign policy interest and intervention. The following examination of some of the major U.S. interventions since the Korean War reveals the great extent to which naked economic interests were of decisive importance.

One of the most significant as well as blatant and continuing American interventions took place in the early

1950s in Iran, which historically had been the exclusive preserve of the British oil industry. In mid-1951 the Anglo-Iranian Oil Company (later British Petroleum), 51 percent of which was owned by the British government and the sole operator in Iran, was nationalized by the Mossadegh government as the Shah fled.

The long-range factors leading up to the nationalization consisted essentially of a widespread belief among Iranians that they got little benefit from the oil industry, and that without control of it they could not rule their own destinies. Related to this were longstanding grievances over the way Iran, historically a political football between Great Britain and Russia, had been forced or "tricked" into unfair oil agreements. The immediate backdrop to the 1951 crisis was the government's drive to gain greater oil revenues for financing its Seven Year Plan, inaugurated in 1949. By that year Venezuela and Saudi Arabia had already won fifty-fifty profit sharing agreements with the international oil companies, while Iran was still receiving a much smaller share, and Anglo-Iranian was stalling on a change.

Following the nationalization, the U.S. government and the leading American oil companies threw their weight behind a worldwide boycott of Iranian oil exports that was 100 percent effective. The boycott, however, did not succeed in overthrowing the Mossadegh regime because the oil sector was a relatively autonomous island in the Iranian economy, affecting only a small number of Iranians; moreover, owing to its small share of profits the government was not heavily dependent on oil revenues. Therefore, more direct U.S. intervention was necessary.

The study of Wise and Ross on the CIA, while noting that "the British and American government had together decided to mount an operation to overthrow Mossadegh," describes graphically the CIA's crucial role:

> There is no doubt at all that the CIA organized and directed the 1953 coup that overthrew Premier Mohammed Mossadegh and kept Shah Mohammed Reza Pahlevi on his throne. But few Americans know that the coup that toppled the government of Iran was led by a CIA agent who was the grandson of President Theodore Roosevelt.
>
> Kermit "Kim" Roosevelt, also a seventh cousin of President Franklin D. Roosevelt, is still known as "Mr. Iran" around the CIA for his spectacular operation in Teheran more than a decade ago. . . .
>
> One legend that grew up inside the CIA had it that Roosevelt, in the grand Rough Rider tradition, led the revolt against the weeping Mossadegh with a gun at the head of an Iranian tank commander as the column rolled into Teheran.
>
> A CIA man familiar with the Iran story characterized this as "a bit romantic" but said: "Kim did run the operation from a basement in Teheran—not from our embassy." He added admiringly: "It was a real James Bond operation."

The rewards to the U.S. oil companies for their solidarity and the CIA's success were substantial. Following the overthrow of the Iranian government, rather than the oil properties being restored to Anglo-Iranian, a new corporation was given control of them. Forty percent of the shares of this corporation went to the five leading United States international oil companies, who in turn gave one-eighth of their share to eleven other United States companies. As a footnote to the whole Iranian affair, Kim Roosevelt subsequently left the CIA, and became Gulf Oil's director of "government relations" in its Washington office.

Again, in 1954, as has now been widely acknowledged

by top U.S. officials, the CIA planned, financed, and provided the arms for the overthrow of the mildly radical Arbenz regime in Guatemala. In 1953 the Arbenz government had dared to expropriate 234,000 acres of uncultivated land owned by United Fruit, offering to compensate the company with bonds payable in twenty-five years. Unfortunately for the Guatemalan government, United Fruit was the dominant factor in the Guatemalan economy, controlling the crucial business of banana production and exports as well as the country's principal railroad. To make things worse, the previous Guatemalan government had alienated U.S. oil companies with a law providing that only companies with majority indigenous ownership could explore for oil within Guatemala, and no crude oil could be exported; as a result, American oil companies withdrew from Guatemalan exploration.

The U.S. government claimed the coup was triggered by the danger of Soviet penetration of the Western Hemisphere. According to Secretary of State John Foster Dulles there was an attempt by "the Guatemalan government and communist agents throughout the world to obscure the real issue . . . —that of communist imperialism—by claiming that the United States is only interested in protecting American business." It is instructive, however, as to the true U.S. motivation that before the CIA enlisted Castillo Armas to lead the military expedition which overthrew the Guatemalan government, it first offered the job to anticommunist exile Miguel Ydigoras Fuentes. He said he turned down the offer for the following reasons:

A former executive of the United Fruit Company, now retired, Mr. Walter Turnbull, came to see me with two gentlemen whom he introduced as agents of the CIA. They said that I was a popular figure in Guatemala and that they wanted to lend their assistance to overthrow Arbenz. When I asked their conditions for the assistance I found them unacceptable. Among other things, I was to promise to favor the United Fruit Company and the International Railways of Central America; to destroy the railroad workers labor union; . . . to establish a strong-arm government, on the style of Ubico. . . .

Moreover, it would be difficult indeed for Secretary of State Dulles not to see danger in the Guatemalan situation. For many years, he had been a stockholder, director, and corporate counsel for United Fruit, and had helped draw up its 1930 and 1936 contracts with this "strong-arm" government of Ubico.

In any event, the new government installed by the CIA proved most accommodating to major U.S. corporate interests. Almost immediately all the land that the Arbenz government had taken from United Fruit was restored to it. Within six months the country's oil laws were changed to allow crude oil exports, and half the area of Guatemala was quickly thrown open for oil concessions. So little attempt was made to veil the real power behind the new government that these oil laws were drafted in English and presented to the Guatemalan Congress for approval in that form; only the request of one deputy who still retained a bit of dignity led to their being translated into Spanish! For U.S. corporations this was a happy ending to the Guatemalan events. Coming hard on the heels of the CIA's success in Iran, it established the efficacy of this type of operation for serving corporate interests.

However, there are times when such operations will not turn the trick and the old tactics of "gunboat diplomacy" are required. This is true in the case of the first open military intervention by the United States since the Korean

War, which again involved crucial corporate interests in Middle Eastern oil. When in the summer of 1958 a military group overthrew the feudal dictatorship in Iraq, the entire Middle East was in ferment. American marines and a naval armada were dispatched to Lebanon, where a civil war threatened, and British paratroopers landed in Jordan. Despite the American government's claim that it sent the marines to protect Lebanon from "foreign agents," there is no question but that oil interests were the precipitating force. Sir Anthony Eden wrote afterward, "Since the United Nations observers were already on the spot and proclaiming that the motives for Anglo-American intervention did not exist, it was rather more heinous."

Indeed, according to the New York *Herald Tribune,* at first the American government gave "strong consideration" to "military intervention to undo the *coup* in Iraq"; the State Department advised the U.S. Ambassador to Lebanon that "marines, starting to land in Lebanon, might be used to aid loyal Iraqi troops to counter-attack." Unfortunately for the United States, no Iraqis could be found to act as tools for restoring a universally detested regime.

Nevertheless, the threat to the new government was clear. *The New York Times* reported the decision of conferences between President Eisenhower, Dulles, and Foreign Secretary Lloyd of Britain: "Intervention will not be extended to Iraq as long as the revolutionary government in Iraq respects Western oil interests." As political scientist Robert Engler comments, "This gunboat diplomacy was clearly in line with the State Department's commitment to pipelines and profits." What other position could be expected from corporate lawyer Dulles, who during the 1956 Suez crisis, declared to a secret meeting of top oil company executives and government officials that as regards U.S. oil holdings in the Middle East *"nationalization of this kind of an asset* impressed with international interest was far beyond compensation of shareholders alone and *should call for international intervention."* Nevertheless, the continuity of American policy can be seen from the fact that the new Iraqi government of Colonel Kassem was overthrown in early 1963 by another *coup.* This *coup* followed right on the heels of Kassem's announcement of the formation of a state oil company to exploit oil lands seized from the companies in 1961; it came four days after Kassem revealed an American note threatening Iraq with sanctions unless he changed his position. He did not, and the Paris weekly *L'Express* stated flatly that "The Iraqi *coup* was inspired by the CIA."

In the same year as the Lebanese intervention the U.S. government, through the CIA, had been covertly involved in supporting Sumatran rebels against Sukarno's government in oil-rich Indonesia. Sukarno had recently swung to the left, and had expropriated most Dutch-owned private property, requested Soviet arms, and brought the Communists into his new coalition government. According to Wise and Ross:

. . . many in the CIA and the State Department saw merit in supporting these dissident elements. Even if Sukarno were not overthrown, they argued, it might be possible for Sumatra, Indonesia's big oil producer, to secede, thereby protecting private American and Dutch holdings.

While this attempt, which included providing planes and pilots to the rebels, failed, the continuing American aim of getting rid of Sukarno was capped with success in the bloodbath of 1966.

Again, the continuing covert and overt U.S. intervention and hostility to the Cuban government clearly had its origins in economic interests. When the Castro government in mid-1959 promulgated an agrarian reform law that threatened U.S. land holdings, according to the *Wall Street Journal* this "crystallized American opposition here [Cuba] to Prime Minister Castro." A year later the point of no return was reached when the Cuban government seized the oil refineries of Jersey, Texaco, and Shell for their refusal to handle Soviet crude oil which the Cubans had bartered for sugar; in almost instant retaliation the U.S. government ended the Cuban sugar quota, and the Cubans in turn seized all American investments in the country. This set the stage for vigorous U.S. attempts to depose Castro, first by economic embargo and then by force of arms at the Bay of Pigs. The oil companies themselves tried singlehandedly to topple the government by threatening to boycott tanker owners carrying Soviet oil to Cuba, an attempt labeled by *The New York Times* as "a unique venture into private foreign policy."

Finally, the last major blatant intervention aside from Vietnam was the landing of U.S. marines in the Dominican Republic to block the accession of former President Juan Bosch in 1965. Bosch had courted U.S. hostility two years earlier when, following his election as president, he began looking to Europe for development funds as a way of reducing his country's dependency upon the United States. One of Bosch's first acts was to sign a $150 million agreement for a hydroelectric project with a Swiss consortium, rather than with U.S. controlled institutions such as the World Bank and the Inter-American Development Bank. Even more significant, as reported in 1963 by journalist I.F. Stone:

Bosch also touched a tender nerve when he complained that the Council of State which ruled the country before the elections had secretly concluded a contract with Standard Oil [Jersey] for a refinery on terms unfavorable to the Dominican Republic. Bosch said he had received better offers in Europe and had warned Standard Oil that the contract would be reviewed as soon as he took office. Bosch said he did so although he knew "my attitude would be used in spreading throughout the world the report that I am hostile to foreign private investments in this country, that I am a Communist, that I am a Fidelista, or that I am something else still more radical." The President elect's prediction proved correct. Though little has appeared in the U.S. press about the Standard Oil contract, a campaign to picture Bosch as somehow linked to Communists has already begun, though he and his entourage are—like most Socialists elsewhere—passionately anti-Communist and anti-Castro.

It should now be clear that frequent U.S. intervention in the underdeveloped world has had a major economic interest. Moreover, as I have tried to show in my book, *The Political Economy of International Oil and the Underdeveloped Countries,* these overt interventions are just the tip of the iceberg; below the surface U.S. governmental power is constantly being used to promote corporate interests abroad. Lest the reader believe that my experience in the international oil industry has led me to overemphasize its significance, it may be helpful to realize that in the third world as a whole, oil investments are the largest U.S. investment. While oil accounts for 40 percent of all U.S. direct investment in the underdeveloped countries, it is so much more profitable than other investments that it makes up 60 percent of all U.S. earnings from such investments. Moreover, since oil wealth is so concentrated in a handful of leading American international companies, it has given them the power virtually to dictate State Department policy in this area. In the words of the late U.S. Senator Neely, "When it comes to matters affecting the profits and self interest of the major oil companies, the oil lobby appears to be more powerful than the President, the Congress, and the people."

This is not to say that narrow economic interests are always the major determinant of U.S. foreign policy. Clearly, our investments and trade with South Korea were far less than the cost of fighting the Korean War. The same is even more true in the case of Vietnam. But, to appreciate the broad significance of economic interests in setting foreign policy one first has to understand the corporate mentality, as clearly expressed in 1965 by Chase Manhattan Bank's vice-president for Far Eastern operations:

In the past, foreign investors have been somewhat wary of the over-all political prospect for the [Southeast Asia] region. I must say, though, that the U.S. actions in Vietnam this year— which have demonstrated that the U.S. will continue to give effective protection to the free nations of the region—have considerably reassured both Asian and Western investors. In fact, I see some reason for hope that the same sort of economic growth may take place in the free economies of Asia that took place in Europe after the Truman Doctrine and after NATO provided a protection shield. The same thing also took place in Japan after the U.S. intervention in Korea removed investor doubts.

One has also to take into account that from the corporate viewpoint it is not correct simply to compare the money cost of an overseas intervention with the profits of U.S. companies from that particular country. Instead one should compare these profits to the real costs to the corporate community of such an intervention. In many cases these real costs are negative, because, for example, with an underemployed economy the spurt to business from the war increases corporate profits; or because even if the real costs are high they are worth the deterrent effect on other countries that might threaten U.S. corporate profits.

Because of gross miscalculations about the ease of winning the Vietnam War, what was initially a profitable stimulant to the corporate economy has now become a great burden. Thus, the overheated war economy generated inflationary pressures that skyrocketed corporate borrowing costs to record levels, put upward pressure on wages, and generated internal discontent. Finally, the Vietnam- induced inflation triggered tremendous European financial pressure on the United States to end the war in order to protect the value of Europe's vast dollar holdings.

It is ironic that post-World War II United States foreign intervention, which started with a broken Europe and then moved to the underdeveloped world, is now receiving blows from both areas. Not only is the United States being beaten by a small but tenacious country in the underdeveloped world, but also by its "allies" in the developed world who themselves had been built up by earlier U.S. interventions. In any event, it seems to me that the focus of American foreign policy is likely to shift increasingly from underdeveloped Asia to the developed world. For one thing, in the last two decades U.S. investment in the developed countries has increased almost ten fold (compared to a tripling in the underdeveloped countries), to a point where it now constitutes three-fourths of the American empire. At the same time the resurrection of continental Europe and Japan now poses an economic challenge that threatens the most vital U.S. interests both in developed and underdeveloped countries. At stake is no less a matter than the financial stability of the international capitalist system and the United States itself. This argument will be detailed later when I discuss the economic crises of the sick society. Now, however, I turn to an examination of the second major disease in the United States today, the problem of black poverty.

4

BLACK POVERTY

To understand the relationship between the corporate economy and the poverty of black people in America today, it is necessary first to recognize that black (and white) poverty is widespread throughout the "affluent society." Even by the Bureau of Labor Statistic's incredibly low "poverty line" of $3,550 per year income for a family of four, 35 percent of all blacks are "poor," compared to 10 percent of all whites. Forty-four percent of all blacks live in substandard housing, compared to 13 percent of all whites.

Thanks partly to the works of people like Gabriel Kolko and Michael Harrington, this situation has gained widespread attention, and even the U.S. government has become officially cognizant with its "antipoverty program." The public airing of the magnitude of this ugly problem— the opening of the eyes of Harvard professors to Roxbury's sores, the entrance of Harlem's smells into air-conditioned Penn Central club cars—is a positive step forward. It is, however, only a part of the battle, and a small part indeed. The really critical question is to what extent racial poverty can be overcome in the corporate society as it exists today.

Existing analyses of racial discrimination and poverty can be divided into two basic groups. First there are what I have come to view as the "My-my" studies, which tell the reader in more or less gory detail the grim facts about Negro poverty. While their styles range from compassion to the dry prose of the U.S. Bureau of Labor Statistics, the thrust is generally the same: "My, my, what a bad situation." Second, there are what I characterize as the "My-my plus math" studies. These run along the lines of stating that there are close to twenty-five million Negroes in America whose average income is $1,000 a year less than whites. By simple arithmetic it becomes "obvious" that all you have to do to end the economic poverty of black people is to increase their income by $25 billion per year—a drop in the bucket for an economy which has reached the stratosphere of a trillion dollar GNP. Here is an example of this thinking:

The U.S. has arrived at the point where poverty could be abolished easily and simply by a stroke of the pen. To raise every individual and family in the nation now below a subsistence income to the subsistence level would cost about $10 billion a year. This is less than 2 percent of the gross national product. It is less than 10 percent of tax revenues. It is about one-fifth of the cost of national defense.

Such an assertion, however, simply points out the arithmetic of poverty and says nothing about whether its abolition or even substantial mitigation can take place within the existing economic, political, social, and psychological structure of American society today. The implication of such thinking is that since we spend $25 billion a year on the Vietnam War, the ending of that war could free us financially to eliminate racial poverty. In arithmetic theorizing this may be true, but it can be of little solace to the black and the poor. A similar argument could have been made even more strongly about the possibilities for ending all poverty after World War II when close to half of the GNP was devoted to the war effort. Far more relevant to the question of the sick society's ability to deal with its racial poverty cancer is the view of President Nixon that "poverty will not be defeated by a stroke of a pen signing a check." Since Nixon is a perfect example of the corporate mentality at work, his indication of writer's cramp in this racial area leaves little room for optimism.

My aim is to develop a more realistic approach to analyzing the problem of black poverty and its prospects for solution. To do this, "white studies" are required rather than "black studies." I propose to start by examining the diverse beneficiaries of racial discrimination who are largely outside the national corporate economy and who provide the major barriers to racial change; and then I will assess the willingness and ability of the national corporate economy to bring its power to bear to overcome these local vested interests.

It is widely agreed that in order to overcome black poverty, we need to destroy racial discrimination in the interrelated areas of jobs, housing, and education. Jobs and housing are the most crucial sectors, since poor education is largely a function of low income and residential segregation. Providing jobs for blacks theoretically falls within the sphere of the corporate economy and the federal government on which it has strong influence. Housing, however, is an area around which there cluster a constellation of powerful local forces that benefit from the existence of black ghettos. It is this sector that we must examine in depth in order to understand the major economic beneficiaries of racial discrimination, as well as their powers to block change.

Before undertaking this analysis, however, it is worth noting that even outside of the housing area there are many whites who benefit to some degree from racial discrimination. This is particularly true in their relation to blacks as suppliers of labor.

Who are these white beneficiaries of discrimination against blacks in the labor market? First there are major corporations, particularly in the South and in "agro-business," which benefit greatly from the cheap labor of blacks, e.g., the lumber mills, the cotton processors, and the tobacco factories. Then there are the smaller businesses, particularly in the North, in the garment industry and in miscellaneous manufacturing, which profit from black labor; for example, Michael Harrington describes the small factory in Chicago, making artificial Christmas trees, nonunion, paying a dollar an hour and no fringe benefits: "The Christmas-tree shop hired Negroes only. That was because they were available cheap; that was because they could be 'kept in their place.' "

Another set of white beneficiaries is the service companies, ranging from the major hotels down to the local greasy spoon diner, which profit from a vast army of low-paid black janitors, chambermaids, dishwashers, etc. In fact, all businesses that need service functions of a menial nature—ranging from the railroads with their porters to every office building with its washroom employees—benefit to some extent from cheap and exploited black labor. For, after all, orthodox economics tells us that in a free and competitive labor market the wage for any job will be relatively high the greater the unwillingness of workers to undertake it and the greater the productivity of the work. Clearly, many of the low-paid occupations that are so brutally spoken of as "nigger work" should by these criteria have a high wage. Very few workers want to clean toilets, and at the same time the productivity of this work is extremely high, as it would be hard to imagine a modern office building functioning with stuffed drains. The fact that racial discrimination creates a huge pool of unemployed blacks who know that thanks to discrimination they have little opportunity for other kinds of work plays a major role in keeping the wage rates for these menial jobs as incredibly low as they are.

Another beneficiary group is the largest single employer of black females—white families in which the women are able to work outside of the home because black females run their households and raise their children. These millions of white women encompass a great range, from teachers and professionals in the North to factory workers in the South. A classic example highlighting this relationship involved the white female textile worker in Montgomery, Alabama who discharged her black female housekeeper for refusing to ride the bus during the black community's historic 1956 bus boycott. The textile worker then quickly had to rehire her black domestic because without the latter's willingness to work for fifteen dollars a week she could not continue to earn her forty dollars a week in the textile mill.

Last, but certainly not least among the beneficiaries of

discrimination are the U.S. armed forces, which find young black men an eager source of cheap labor. While blacks make up about 10 percent of the population, they account for close to 20 percent of the combat troops in Vietnam. They make up an even higher proportion of the elite fighting units such as the paratroops and airborne rifle platoons. Moreover, as a *New York Times* series on the role of the Negro soldier in Vietnam pointed out, the young black men recruited into Vietnam are often particularly "good" soldiers, since they can release in war the bottled up anger of living in a racist society. Despite his high fatality rate, opportunities for the black man in the army are so much better than his prospects as a civilian that in 1966 two-thirds of all first-term black soldiers reenlisted; this compares with a reenlistment rate for whites of only one-fifth. There could be no more eloquent comment on racism in the sick society than that of a black civilian working in Vietnam, who said he was there for "bread and freedom, man, bread and freedom."

Turning now to the crucial housing sector, we shall see that virtually all forces operating there have a vested interest in preventing effective action for alleviating the plight of the black community. At the center of the opposition to change are the slum real estate owners. In analyzing the crucial stake of "slum-lords" in discrimination we are aided by George Sternlieb's study, *The Tenement Landlord*. Sternlieb made an intensive analysis of over 500 slum tenements in Newark, New Jersey. The wealth of data uncovered in this study explodes many myths about slum ownership, and reveals that the problem is far more intractable than many believe.

The first important finding is that while both whites and blacks live in slums, slum housing in black ghettos is much more profitable. The census data for 1960 show that in Newark's predominantly black ghetto, the average monthly rent paid by nonwhites was seventy-six dollars, or one-sixth more than the average rents in Newark's white slums; at the same time the quality of black housing was inferior to that of whites. Furthermore, this differential is lower than that found in Chicago, where blacks paid almost one-third more than whites for their slums.

Moreover, most of the costs of owning and operating slum housing, like any other housing, are relatively fixed. These high fixed costs mean that a reduction in rent revenues of a given percentage would reduce profits by a multiple of that percentage. Thus, a reduction of the rent levels of black housing on the order of 20 percent would cause typical slum-lord profits to drop not by one-fifth but by three-fourths. (This is totally analogous to the phenomenon discussed in the last chapter, where the profits of U.S. corporations are far more heavily dependent on foreign sales than would appear; the common cause is the existence of high fixed costs.)

In short, if black slum housing were reduced in rent to the level of comparable white housing, the "superprofits" derived by landlords from black slum tenements would be wiped out. Some idea of the total magnitude of the slum landlord's stake in discrimination may be gleaned from the following figures. According to Bureau of Labor Statistics studies, urban blacks spend over 10 percent of their incomes on rental housing, or an aggregate $3 billion per year. Assuming that blacks pay "only" 20 percent more rent because of discrimination, this amounts to about $500 million per year. This is indeed a sizable vested interest by any standard.

The large size of the white stake in black slum ownership is particularly important in light of a second factor that Sternlieb's study demonstrates: slum owners are far more numerous than is generally believed. The problem of slum ownership is not simply that of a few rich landlords, but of many people from various walks of life having a vested interest in discrimination. In the black area studied in Newark, one-third of all the tenements (most of which had only three to six apartments) were owned by people who possessed only one tenement; another quarter of the total was owned by those with two to three tenements.

Real estate agents are another crucial group that joins forces with slum owners to oppose alleviation of the plight of blacks in the housing area. The views of real estate agents (of which there are 150,000 in America), as expressed by the National Association of Real Estate Boards (NAREB) and various local boards, have until recently been strongly against nondiscriminatory housing laws; these have been labeled by them "forced housing laws." Only after the June 1968 Supreme Court decision declaring open housing to be the law of the land has NAREB reversed its position; local real estate boards, however, which wield the real power, are likely to be as unreconstructed as ever.

At the same time, real estate boards are strongly opposed to government slum clearance programs. Ostensibly this is because they feel that private enterprise can do the job just as well. Whether or not this is true, there is no question that government slum clearance and public housing are direct threats to the real estate agent's livelihood. Real estate agents cannot get fees for finding tenants for public housing since anyone can apply directly; nor can they get fees for managing the properties, which are normally run by government employees. In addition, to the extent that low-cost public housing allows blacks to escape from slum housing, they lower the profits of the many real estate agents who own such housing. In the long run, the large-scale spread of public housing could seriously encroach on the realtor's business.

The opposition of real estate agents and their boards to changes for blacks is particularly crucial because of their enormous and widespread local power, for housing is preeminently a local industry. Studies by Donald Bouma, which intensively analyze the role of a particularly effective real estate board in a Midwestern city, bare the bases of real estate board power. Among these are expertise in the complicated field of housing, as well as solid standing in the community. Moreover, the real estate agent who has frequent contact with a large number of people in the community is seen by them not as a "big shot" leader, but as an average citizen: "A newspaper editor said that the 'board has an advantage over the Chamber of Commerce in that the latter is associated with money, and that develops antagonisms among the workingmen.' "

In addition, real estate boards have become masters at shrouding their narrow self-interest in the flag of the general good; their fight is not against good housing, but for private home ownership, low taxes, and "the American Way of Life" in general. In line with this approach, real estate boards are very adept at working through other groups to achieve their aims. Thus, in 1964 the National Association of Real Estate Boards prepared a kit of materials on "forced housing" for its local members, which it was hoped "will be of help to you in opposing the type of legislation detrimental to our real estate profession as well as to the human right of property ownership." Among the documents sent out was a "Suggested Procedure for Organizing a Civic Association or Property Owners Organization," which details the techniques for creating front groups:

. . . The efforts of any group will be of much greater effect if the group represents a wide range of interests and occupations and is not dominated by the Real Estate Board.

A Civic Association or Property Owners Organization is in a much better position to spearhead the education of the public about the dangers of trying to legislate the complicated question of minority housing. . . .

In the organizational stages of one of these Associations it is important that the real estate man lend what help he can without tending to take over the organization. He should be as much in the background as is possible. . . .

The best way to form the group is to get the leaders of the community together. . . .

. . . Civic leaders such as are in the Lions, Kiwanis, Legion, VFW, DAV, etc., are the people to try to get to the first meeting. A Civic Association may get into areas of discussion and interest that none of the above mentioned organizations can. This makes the Civic Association a non-partisan and non-sectarian organization. It makes the Civic Association a watch-dog of the community.

How these tactics can work out in practice is documented by Bouma. In fights against public housing the real estate board joined with local builders and building supply dealers to form an "Allied Construction and Real Estate Council," which successfully defeated the public housing bill and then was allowed to lapse. But, so great is a real estate board's influence, it can often win even when standing alone. In one case of a referendum on public housing, the real estate board was opposed by the chamber of commerce, the county council of churches and thirty-two affiliated organizations, social welfare groups, unions, and the two daily newspapers, yet the real estate board won by a three to two margin.

As noted, real estate agents look to assistance from builders and developers in their opposition to non-discriminatory housing. Usually they are opposed to open housing laws, partly because they fear that if they accept blacks in a new development it will be difficult to sell additional housing to whites. At the same time, they are opposed to traditional public housing programs. Public housing not only eliminates a potential area for private profit, but by increasing the total supply of housing may reduce the profitability of new or planned private housing.

The real estate boards and the builders are the spearheads of opposition to better black housing. But their efforts would not be nearly so successful were they not allied with much larger white forces which also have an economic stake in the status quo. Thus, workers in the lily-white construction trades make up six percent of the U.S. labor force. These workers have strong economic incentives to keep blacks out of the construction unions; these white guild craftsmen often want to pass along their relatively high paying jobs to their sons, and also prevent an expansion of the supply of construction labor which would tend to slow the rise in their wages. Further, so long as construction demand is relatively high they have little interest in public housing, and strongly oppose any use of nonunion black labor to lower the cost of building ghetto housing.

Even more important, the majority of white Americans are home owners and their house is by far their most important economic asset. One of their greatest fears is that the entry of blacks into their neighborhood, whether in private or public housing, will drive down property values because whites will flee. This makes most homeowners strong allies of the real estate agents and builders in their fight against nondiscriminatory housing.

The currently fashionable view is that the problems of black housing will ultimately be solved by governmental power overcoming those with a vested interest in housing discrimination and black ghettos. Evidence that this is a delusion can be seen from the tortured history of public housing in the sick society, as detailed by Leonard Freedman in *Public Housing: The Politics of Poverty*.

This case study is particularly relevant as blacks constitute a majority of public housing occupants. It illustrates how, in the absence of a strong national corporate will to solve a problem, the combination of powerful local economic groups and a political structure oriented to the status quo can easily block change.

During World War II, in response to the corporate economy's need for housing war production workers, the government found the resources for a "massive program" of public housing; while most of it was temporary, over 170,000 new permanent units were constructed. After the war, with private housing taking care of the needs of the middle and upper classes, the corporate urge for government housing weakened drastically. Nevertheless, in 1949, after a five-year struggle, congressional legislation was passed authorizing 810,000 new public housing units to be built over a period of six years. In fact, the last of these units was still not completed twenty years later. As a result, public housing now accounts for a mere 1 percent of all housing in the United States as compared to 20 percent in Great Britain.

What are the reasons for this situation? A key sponsor of the 1949 legislation was Republican Senator Robert A. Taft, whose devotion to corporate capitalism cannot be challenged. As an enlightened conservative, however, he recognized that it was necessary to have some minimum federal government intervention for the poor, particularly in this area because "private development and perfectly free enterprise in the United States . . . has never eliminated those slums and I see no reason to think that they ever will, because they simply cannot reach the lowest income group." Nevertheless, Taft appeared to have been ahead of his time. In the 1950s and early 1960s when ghetto uprisings were not a major threat, the corporate community was cool if not outrightly hostile to public housing. Among the groups that worked against it were the U.S. Chamber of Commerce, the Mortgage Bankers Association of America, the American Bankers Association, the National Association of Lumber Manufacturers, and the Building Products Institute. One reason was that in America, publicly owned housing means subsidized housing. These subsidies ultimately come from the general taxes, including those paid by the corporate community. Additionally, some corporations feared public housing as establishing a precedent for government entry into competition with private business.

This situation made public housing a sitting duck for the primarily local opposition groups, which included most of the people directly or indirectly engaged in building, selling, or financing housing. According to Freedman, three of these groups played a crucial role in watering down the public housing program. These were NAREB; the National Association of Homebuilders, an offshoot of NAREB whose 40,000 members make up 85 percent of the country's home builders; and the United States Savings and Loan League, whose 5,000 members include most of the savings and loan associations throughout the country. (As the reader should recall, congressmen are particularly active in savings and loan associations.) Freedman summarizes how these groups took advantage of our peculiar political structure to emasculate public housing over the years:

Arrayed against public housing was a coalition of groups peculiarly well equipped to take advantage of the opportunities for obstruction provided by the legislative process. The private housing organizations, particularly the realtors, the home builders, and the savings and loan leagues, were singled out by a congressional committee investigating lobbying practices in 1950 as being especially skillful and resourceful in their pressure tactics. For one thing, they employed able, experienced staffs in Washington who knew how to move around in the labyrinthine windings of the legislative process. With party leadership relatively weak, congressional power is fragmented; determined, nationally organized groups who know what they want and persist in trying to get it are in a good position to benefit from the diffusion of legislative authority. Facing a system that contains innumerable "points of access," the private housing groups have known at what points and at what times they must apply their pressure.

Even more important, the structure of the private housing organizations enabled them to seize upon the most characteristic feature of the congressman's behavior—his tendency to respond to influences from his home district. It happened to be the case that each of the private housing organizations, while maintaining a national structure, was made up of local units that wielded considerable influence in most of the communities where new public housing projects were proposed. This made it possible for the anti-public housing groups both to coordinate local pressures on Congress and to play an important supporting role in many of the local campaigns.

One irony of the situation is that despite the private housing industry's outcry against public housing as "a government handout," it, like many other industries, has been a great beneficiary of government support. This has been particularly true with regard to government underwriting of housing credit, for through the Veteran's Administration and the Federal Housing Administration, the government has contributed vitally to the growth of the private housing industry. Given this, one can readily understand housing expert Charles Abrams' conclusion that the private housing industry favors "socialism for the rich and free enterprise for the poor."

The second major group that derives direct economic benefits from racial discrimination is the ghetto merchants. This has been carefully documented in a study by David Caplovitz, appropriately entitled *The Poor Pay More,* which deals with marketing in New York City's slums. The slum consumer is trapped in the ghetto by a combination of economic constraints and psychological fears that act to restrict his mobility. At the same time his consumer ignorance makes him an attractive victim for sharp selling practices. To complete the circle, as sociological studies have shown, the poor, blocked from occupational mobility and advancement, compensate psychologically by consuming beyond their means. These consumption pressures have undoubtedly greatly increased since television has brought into every ghetto home constant reminders of what the good life is like, or is supposed to be like, in white, suburban America.

Not surprisingly then, to the ghetto merchant the local consumer is seen as prey:

People do not shop in this area. Each person who comes into the store wants to buy something and is a potential customer. It is just up to who catches him!

One key to high profitability for ghetto merchants is that given the knowledge that they are not competing with non-ghetto stores, they can charge very high prices for inferior quality goods. The typical markup above the wholesale price is between 100 and 300 percent; very often there are no set prices and the merchant simply charges what he thinks he can get from each customer. Gouging of the slum dweller is also practiced by national food chains. A recent comprehensive study by the Federal Trade Commission found that, owing to the lack of competition within the ghetto, chain food stores charge up to 10 percent more in slums than in other areas.

Some of the shady marketing practices, such as "switch sales," used to further milk the consumer, apparently astound some of the ghetto merchants themselves. As one stated to Caplovitz:

I don't know how they do it. They advertise three rooms of furniture for $149 and the customers swarm in. They [the customers] end up buying a $400 bedroom set for $600 and none of us can believe how easy it is to make these sales.

Leaving aside such disarming modesty, all ghetto merchants know that the ultimate key to the ghetto consumer's ability to pay these exorbitant prices is credit. Of fourteen merchants interviewed in Caplovitz's study, twelve did more than three-quarters of their business on credit. Seventy-seven percent of all black families in the ghettos use credit, and not only is credit used to get the consumer to make the initial purchase, but it is also a method used to "hook" the ghetto consumer into making further purchases.

Merchants try particularly hard to make a sale to a customer when he is nearing the end of debt payments for his previous purchases, thereby seeking to emulate the southern plantation store-sharecropper relationship.

Since credit is crucial to ghetto profitability, ghetto merchants have developed an elaborate collection system. In many places they can threaten to get a lien against property or to garnishee the wages of their customers. Because many employers will fire workers rather than bother with the bookkeeping of garnishment this is a potent threat against a worker in debt. Again, while it is not possible to attach welfare payments, because welfare families are not supposed to buy on credit, the merchant's threat of reporting these credit purchases to the Welfare Department is another powerful weapon. An additional instrument of control is the Credit Association ratings; a bad rating by one merchant threatens to cut off all potential credit purchases by the slow ghetto payer. It is instructive that the normal method of guaranteeing credit payments, the threat of repossession, is of relatively little use to the ghetto merchant other than as a deterrent, because the merchandise is frequently so shoddy that it is hardly worth reclaiming.

The ghetto merchant is a significant obstacle to eliminating black poverty because he is directly dependent for his living on the very existence of the ghetto. Any plans for slum clearance threaten his business, often literally, because in the ghettos the homes of the poor and the stores they shop in frequently occupy the same building. The ghetto merchant is often a powerful force on the local scene, since he is a substantial property owner who by the nature of his business is tied to the police, the courts, and local political leaders.

It is extremely important to realize that the ghetto merchant's power to maintain the status quo is buttressed by the broad community of interests many major national corporations share with him. Part of the common interests derive from little known links between the prestigious national corporations and the disreputable ghetto merchants. For one thing, ghetto credit is just one link in a vast credit chain that supports marketing throughout the United States. The credit structure is like a ladder with steps of relative risk and knowledgeability of the credit customers, each step associated with a higher interest cost. At the base would be the commercial bank loans to their most trustworthy and shrewd customers, the major corporations, who pay the prime rate, normally about 6 percent. Next come the bank loans to individuals, which may cost 8-12 percent, followed by merchandise credit at 18 percent, finance company small loans at up to 36 percent, and finally the loan sharks who charge 200-300 percent or more. The ghetto dweller is a particularly profitable credit source because he normally has to borrow from the highest-priced credit sources, e.g., twice as many blacks borrow from finance companies as from banks. But many of the respectable institutions on the ladder benefit from the ghetto dweller since they lend in turn to the more "shady" companies that deal with him directly.

The fact that credit sales are (as we shall discuss in detail later) crucial to the American economy means that the major corporations who wield national power will be very reluctant to lobby against the usurious credit practices of ghetto merchants. Indeed, it took years of struggle by liberal forces to obtain a "Truth in Lending" Act which merely requires that the consumer be told what are the true interest costs of borrowing, e.g., that 1.5 percent per month means 18 percent per year. (Not surprisingly, reports indicate that consumers are indifferent to this information; all they care about is the size of the monthly payments necessary to buy the goods.)

Furthermore, the deception that ghetto merchants perpetrate on their customers is frequently aided and abetted by the biggest corporations in pursuit of their own profits. For example, home-improvement frauds are one of the biggest areas of consumer deception in the country as a whole, but are particularly widespread and injurious in the ghettos. According to the attorney in charge of prosecuting home-improvement frauds at the Federal Trade Commission, large finance houses and large building materials corporations aid and abet the small operators who directly cheat the poor. These big corporations have not only supplied the fraudulent operators with inferior products, but assisted them in their credit plans, advertising, and promotion. Yet nothing significant has been done to curb these powerful corporations with their congressional lobbies.

In addition to the direct collusion between big corporations and ghetto merchants, they, as well as slumlords, share a parallelism of interest: maintaining the sanctity of property whose high profits derive from its monopolistic position. Blacks pay more for less because their practical restriction to the urban ghetto derives from white monopoly control of the rest of the economy. Similarly, monopoly control is the central means by which all corporations attempt to achieve goals of profit maximization. From the corporate viewpoint, forcing blacks to purchase goods at higher prices by offering no real alternatives is no different from brainwashing white and black consumers into paying ten times as much for a brand name aspirin that is chemically identical to a nonbrand one. (It is not accidental, although it is perhaps ironic, that the attempt to get the less knowledgeable or weaker buyer to pay more for a product than another buyer is known in business literature as "price discrimination," and has no moral overtones whatsoever.) To paraphrase a popular saying, "Monopoly is as American as cherry pie."

This parallelism of interests in the maintenance of monopoly control is a significant factor in weakening any tendency for the national corporate sector to use its power in overcoming black poverty. Another, albeit relatively minor factor, is the widespread racism that is endemic to a largely lily white world of top corporate executives. This racism often runs so deep that the executive is unaware of it. I vividly recall an official of a major American company bemoaning to a dark-skinned Asian the problems the United States was having with its "niggers." Such prejudices, however, have been and can be quickly suppressed in the modern corporation when they are seen as serious barriers to profit maximization.

Far more significant is the fact that the corporate sector starts out with two serious handicaps to generating pressure for major governmental change to overcome black poverty. First, as in the case of housing, effective government action would frequently be detrimental to corporate profits because it would require subsidies that must be financed by taxes. Second, as we have seen in the case of housing, much of the necessary government action must come from locally controlled political leaders who are least susceptible to control by the national corporate sector.

Given these inhibiting factors, it is not surprising that the corporate sector normally is unwilling and/or unable to force radical government action in this area. Clearly, however, these are not normal times. The 1960s have seen the specter of black power haunting the corporate society. History demonstrates that the threat of mass black power is not readily ignored in the sick society. For example, only A. Philip Randolph's planned mass march on Washington at the outset of World War II forced President Roosevelt to set up a Fair Employment Practices Commission—a commission that was killed after the war.

What is new in the present era is that the locus of responsibility for overcoming black poverty has shifted partly from the government to the corporate sector. Thus, in recent years government leaders, corporate officials, and "moderate" black leaders have increasingly stressed the potential role of direct action by major corporations to help end black poverty. As expressed by black educator Kenneth Clark, "Business and industry are our last hope." Numerous top corporate executives have made impressive speeches exhorting their fellow businessmen to recognize the "social responsibility" of business in this area.

Despite the fog of words, however, the critical question is "What are the realistic prospects for these words to be translated into significant actions?" The answer can be drawn from an examination of the relatively recent history of corporate "concern" for the plight of black people in America.

It seems clear that this corporate concern is a response to the increasing militancy of civil rights groups, dating from the 1960 "sit-in" movement. The initial business reactions are clearly indicated in a book entitled *The Management of Racial Integration in Business,* written by Georges Doriot and published in 1963. At the time Mr. Doriot was a professor in Harvard's prestigious Business School; moreover, he commanded great respect in the business community as the founder of a high-powered technology company who had himself made $25 million. Since Mr. Doriot's book is also based on case studies of the actual experiences of numerous corporate executives it can be taken a reliable indicator of corporate thinking at that juncture.

In the very beginning of the book, Mr. Doriot sketches his reasons for believing that racial integration in business is inevitable. The basic factor is the fear that the Negro can so disrupt business as to make integration "a lesser evil." For example, Doriot talks of the capacity of civil rights demonstrators to hurt business by sit-ins, picket lines, tying up telephone lines, etc. He recognizes that given the crucial nature of communications in modern business, even short of using outright violence, the Negro has a serious potential for profit-damaging activities.

Mr. Doriot then goes on to note:

Perhaps because of the difficulty of justifying business decisions on moral grounds, those companies that seemed to emphasize the moral aspects of racial integration generally accomplished the least.

Attacking discrimination within business on moral grounds may make it harder to convince others within of the *practical* need for racial integration.

Lest the reader miss this crucial point of racial integration basically being justifiable in the corporation only in terms of profits, Mr. Doriot makes it crystal clear: "Not yet seeing integration as a pragmatic necessity closely related to profit and loss, and, therefore, not approaching it with the proper thought and careful research, companies assuming the moral tactic often find themselves in contradictory and uncomfortable positions."

Nevertheless, considerable corporate opposition to integration at that time is indicated by some of Doriot's case studies. He notes that most chemical companies, since they are fairly immune from consumer boycotts, have devoted little effort toward integration. One company changed its hiring policy only when it introduced a "hair straightener" for the black market. Then there was the major eastern city bank that was being boycotted by civil rights groups:

As the president of one boycotted bank put it, "I never knew I had so few friends." All his competitors privately encouraged him to fight the Negro demonstrations, while they publicly supported the need for increased integration and hired additional Negroes for *high-visibility* positions in their own firms.

An instructive example of one of the few sizable corporate efforts in the racial area in the early 1960s was the pioneering program of U.S. Gypsum Company. This large manufacturer of building materials entered the arena of private slum renovation in 1964 to the tune of much publicity and loudly proclaimed hopes that here was the ultimate solution to slum housing. U.S. Gypsum's explicitly stated aim was to make money: by originating pilot projects in various cities it hoped to attract other private contractors into slum renovation and thereby provide a market for its building materials. Despite the fact that according to the *Wall Street Journal*, in five years U.S. Gypsum "proceeded only in dribs and drabs," it ran into many difficulties and continually lost money on the project, leading to its recent termination.

The U.S. Gypsum experience has generated considerable disillusionment with the prospects for private sector slum renovation, even when backed by big corporations. One reason is, as the *Wall Street Journal* put it, "Unfortunately, no other big for-profit corporations are busting down U.S. Gypsum's door to buy its building products." One other major corporation, Armstrong Cork, which tested a pilot project by rehabilitating nine slum houses and selling them to low income families, has already discontinued the project after losing $5,000 on each house. It appears that the corporate community increasingly agrees with the views of Mrs. Hortense Gabel, a former New York City Rent and Rehabilitation Administrator (who ironically is credited with drawing U.S. Gypsum into its slum renovation effort):

Big business alone can't clear up the nation's slums. There is no way to fix up rotting buildings and improve the upward job mobility and stake in society of the people who live in them without massive infusions of federal money.

The corporate community showed no real sense of urgency about the black problem until the devastating Watts uprising of 1965, and even more, the widespread upheavals of 1967. Concrete evidence of this is available from a 1969 management survey of 250 of the country's largest corporations. As reported in the *Harvard Business Review,* the survey showed that 80 percent of giant corporations now have some kind of program for assisting ghetto blacks, compared to less than 2 percent before 1965.

Suddenly, for many major companies the danger was no longer annoying picketing and sit-ins, but the destruction of their corporate plant and equipment from whence all profits flow. A blatant and significant example of this new corporate concern is described in *Fortune*'s January 1968 special issue on "Business and the Urban Crisis" (itself a response to the urban uprisings):

One night last July, James M. Roche, then the president (and now the chairman) of General Motors Corp., was working late on the fourteenth floor of the G.M. Building in Detroit. As he was mulling over the affairs of Chevrolet, Pontiac, Oldsmobile, Buick, Cadillac, Delco, Frigidaire, Electro Motive, and the rest, he was disturbed by an eerie flickering. He looked out to see his city in flames—"I never thought I would see anything like that." Since then, with a group of fellow Detroiters of equal stature . . . Roche has made "the city" his most urgent business.

[Three months later] G.M. Chairman James Roche himself flew up to Lansing to plead the cause of open housing before an unenthusiastic legislature.

The first organized corporate response to the devastating 1967 uprisings appeared in the famous U.S. Riot Commission (Kerner) Report, which contained in Appendix H a "Report to the Commission by the advisory panel on private enterprise." The members of this panel were a sampling of top corporate leadership, including the chairman of Litton Industries, the president of North American Rockwell, the chief economist of the Bank of America, and a vicepresident of General Mills. After initial rhetoric such as "We conclude that maximum utilization of the tremendous capability of the American free enterprise system is a crucial element in any program for improving conditions," the advisory panel got down to brass tacks: "We believe that a truly massive number of companies could be induced to participate only if appropriate monetary incentives are provided by the federal government to defray the unusual cost of participation."

More specifically, the advisory group focused on the estimated 500,000 "hard-core" unemployed, seen as the key to the black community's potential for violence. The panel estimated that it costs an employer $3,000 to $5,000 per year to take on such a person as a trainee. The heart of the group's proposal was that business be given major tax credits for undertaking these additional costs: namely, 75 percent of these employee's wages in the first six months,

50 percent in the second six months, and 25 percent in the second year. The panel estimated that over a two-year period these tax credits would amount to about $3,000 per employee, or some $1.5 billion if all of the "hard-core" were employed.

Taking its cue, Congress enacted a subsidy program for job training, in which direct payments to companies average around $3,000 per trainee. The brief history of the Job Opportunities in the Business Sector (JOBS) program reveals clearly the weakness of the corporate will to overcome black poverty, as well as the severe structural handicaps under which the corporate sector labors in this area.

During the first year of the program, through mid-1969, only 77,000 workers had been signed up and only 27,000 were on the job. The National Alliance of Businessmen (NAB), which is spearheading this government-industry effort, claimed that during this period 230,000 hard-core unemployed had been taken on (most without benefit of subsidy), but admitted that only 125,000 were still on the job. Moreover, the NAB has been criticized by the government's General Accounting Office for having shaky data to back up its purported achievements. Thus, despite a combination of government subsidy, major corporate pressure, and the tightest labor market since World War II, by mid-1969 the job training program covered at most one-forth of the hard-core unemployed.

Predictably, the recession that began in late 1969 sharply undercut the JOBS program. Many corporations became increasingly leery of it since they were looking to cut employment, not raise it. Thus, in the fiscal year ending June 1970, the Labor Department paid out only $105 million for the JOBS program, instead of the $420 million originally considered necessary.

The deadliest blow came from Chrysler Corporation, which in early 1970 canceled a commitment made with considerable fanfare a year earlier to train 4,500 production workers under a $14 million government grant. This had been the largest commitment made by any corporation. Ironically, the Chrysler cancellation announcement came several days before its president became the new chairman of the NAB!

Chrysler was not alone in the auto industry, by far the JOBS program's largest employer, in suiting its response to corporate profit needs. As a *Wall Street Journal* reporter noted in the early growth phase of JOBS:

Yet despite the dramatic sweep of Detroit's response, the fact is that the auto makers moved—and continue to move—in an essentially cautious manner. Everything that has been done so far has fallen well within the boundaries of corporate prudence, self interest and profit making—including the lowered hiring standards. When the auto makers started snapping up hard-core unemployed, they were desperately in need of workers in a hurry and the unemployment rolls were skimpy.

In keeping with the overriding dictates of profit making, Ford, which started out as the boldest of the auto makers (Henry Ford is a major leader in the JOBS program), was among the first to retrench its minority employment programs. When Ford's sales slowed so that a production cutback was needed in early 1969, it "quietly closed" its two newly established hiring centers in Detroit's ghettos, and then laid off some of its very recently hired hard-core employees, rejecting a union request to give them preference as "not practical." Little wonder then that a *New York Times* portrait of Henry Ford, noting his reputation as a socially concerned business leader (his friend Whitney Young of the Urban League said, perhaps the only one in

America), points out that "in truth, Ford is not a concerned industrialist, but only what passes for one, especially when his concerns and actions and those of his company are measured against the problems that confront America"; more direct is the comment of community organizer Saul Alinsky, that Ford's urban involvement, like the urban involvement of all big business and big government, "boils down to what I academically call a pile of ——."

The caution of the auto makers has been attributed to a number of factors: fear of stockholder objections, fear of being resented by potential customers if they push too hard into controversial areas, and perhaps even fear of just having too many black workers (particularly in light of the various local unions of "black revolutionaries" formed in the industry). Underlying all of this, however, is the fundamental fact that large corporations are "rational" organizations whose most important goal is to make profits for their stockholders.

Even in the best of times corporate leaders are normally reluctant to allow their efficiency oriented organizations to become infected with "social considerations" that blur the sharp and unambiguous criterion of profit maximization. When the economic winds blow ill, however, all eyes must perforce be focused on the profit goal. Thus, the basic answers to the question posed by a *Wall Street Journal* reporter, "Why can't companies as big and powerful as GM and Ford get over their hangups, harness their influence and move on to bolder and rangier objectives?" were given in *Barron's* prescient warning in July 1968, at the inception of the JOBS program:

By following without demur the lead of the National Alliance of Businessmen, a group of socially conscious top-drawer executives which has pledged to find jobs for a half million "hard core" unemployed by mid-1971, U.S. commerce and industry have struck an equally bad bargain. . . . By urging jobs for the unemployable, it constitutes a naked assault on objective standards of performance and rewards for merit. Finally, with a reckless disregard of risk, financial and political alike, advocates of the private WPA have accepted a heavy (not to say open-end) commitment in good times which a sudden onset of adversity—perhaps like the one that now threatens—may make difficult if not impossible to honor.

At its best the JOBS program accelerated the entry of a relatively small number of blacks into a high-paying industry like automobile production, whose man-killing pace was already creating high absenteeism among whites; the black foothold, however, was extremely tenuous. The pathos of the situation was pointed up in a *New York Times* reporter's interviews with "disappointed" blacks recently hired and fired by the auto industry: "Mr. Robinson said that he liked the job so much and the pay was so good that he didn't mind getting up at 4:30 A.M. to ride 35 miles with a friend and getting home at 5 P.M."

At its worst the program serves to enhance corporate profits while "training" the black for lifelong poverty, as in the government-backed drive to increase the supply of domestic servants. One example reported by the *Washington Post* involved the federal government supplying money for "teaching" black females in La Grange, Georgia to be domestic servants, with a top wage available upon graduation of four dollars per day! This program is clearly a corporate dream, particularly for the Callaway Mills Company, the town's largest employer. The program will allow the company to perpetuate its low pay for white female textile workers who must hire black females to take care of their children while they work in the mill. As one reporter who analyzed this federal subsidy to assist corporate profit-making so aptly put it, "It takes the guts of a burglar to call a sewer like this the Great Society."

The corporate society's newest major program for overcoming black poverty is its widely heralded support for "black capitalism," described by President Nixon as a means of "giving them a piece of the action." The basic concept is to aid the black community by creating black-owned ghetto businesses, which in turn provide employment for other blacks. The growth of black capitalism is envisaged primarily through use of corporate funds and talent, with little money coming directly from the federal government.

The most important mechanism for implementing this approach was to be the Minority Enterprise Small Business Investment Company (MESBIC). The grand dream was for one hundred MESBICs to be sponsored by major corporations (or private groups) by mid-1970. These would generate $500 million in minority business investment—with each corporation putting up merely $150,000! The remaining $485 million would come from matching 2:1 loans from the Federal Small Business Administration, plus the latter's guaranteeing 90 percent of some $450 million to be borrowed by MESBICs from private banks. Alas for the dream, by mid-1970 only nine MESBICs had been organized, and some of them had not even granted any loans.

As with the JOBS program, a basic reason for the failure was the weakness of the corporate commitment to "social goals" when they come into conflict with profit maximization. With interest rates at record highs, many banks were extremely reluctant to tie up their money in the MESBIC program. With major corporations frantically seeking to build up their own liquidity, it is not surprising that there was no great rush to "throw away" money—even $150,000.

In the words of the Under Secretary of Commerce, acknowledging the lag in the black capitalism program, "It's hard to imbue businessmen with social consciousness when business is bad."

It is also probable that corporate zeal for black capitalism has been weakened by the generally bad experiences of the few major corporations that launched their own highly touted assistance programs even before President Nixon got in on the act. An examination of the brief history of one of these efforts reveals clearly the difficulties individual corporations face in this area.

In early 1968 EG&G, Inc., a rapidly growing "technology" science oriented company headquartered in New England, set up a metal fabricating subsidiary in Roxbury, the black ghetto of Boston. The subsidiary was to be staffed by local blacks who would receive full ownership in twenty years.

Unfortunately for those who had great faith in corporate sponsored black capitalism, EG&G's Roxbury experience has been a disaster. One problem was that with an untrained and unskilled black staff, both at the working and managerial levels, the company was unable to compete effectively. Thus, EG&G's preliminary profitability studies indicated that the overhead costs in this plant should normally equal about half of the direct labor cost; in practice, the Roxbury plant overhead turned out to run three times as high as labor cost.

In addition, serious problems were caused by the inability of the new venture to generate the expected volume of sales. As the president of EG&G lamented:

Everybody was hopped up over this thing two years ago. Company presidents would say, "Sure, we'll buy from you." This would be passed down through vice-presidents to the purchasing agent, whose job is to buy at the lowest price. He'd give us $500 to $1,000 worth of business, which is worse than nothing at all. I guess I know what blacks mean when they talk about tokenism.

As a result, EG&G's black subsidiary lost "hundreds of thousands of dollars" in its first nine months of operation. Its regular operations earn less than $5 million per year, and the company has had a rapid growth rate in earnings, enabling its stock to sell at a very high price-earnings multiple. Thus, EG&G was in no position to afford such losses on a continuing basis. Hence, its initial reaction was to cut back by discharging ten of its original seventy-eight black employees.

However, despite this discouraging record, the company continued with the Roxbury project. The reason may lie partly in the company's desire to ingratiate itself with the Atomic Energy Commission. The AEC, which generates a substantial part of the company's $110 million dollars in sales, requires contractors to develop "affirmative action programs" for minority groups. Thus, the *Wall Street Journal* reports:

> William Dilday, one of the black salaried employees laid off at ERI [the EG&G subsidiary] before Christmas, says, "Corporate headquarters used to call down to us to get the numbers of blacks and other minority workers at ERI to include in reports they were preparing for Government contracts. I strongly suspect the major reason for ERI's existence is to help them qualify for Federal contracts under the Fair Employment clauses."
>
> An EG&G official says that while the ERI venture probably hasn't gotten any Federal contracts for the parent company, "It hasn't hurt a bit. The Government looks favorably on what we are trying to do at ERI."

In any event, EG&G's ghetto subsidiary continued to sustain losses in its second year of operation with projections of even further losses for its third year. Meanwhile, the parent company had also suffered other reversals. Its net income dropped from $3.7 million in 1968 to a loss of $2.2 million in 1969, and the price of its stock plunged from $50 to under $10. Therefore, in early 1970 EG&G decided to throw in the towel and close down the Roxbury plant. As a company spokesman said, "We simply had to live up to our responsibility to our shareholders to eliminate the continuing high rate of losses there." In the postmortem period, EG&G's president, somewhat chastened by his experience, particularly the lack of support from other corporations, doubted that his company would try again "though I'll help the next guy who tries." His experience, however, is unlikely to encourage many major corporations to be the "next guy."

Moreover, EG&G's dismal results are likely to be typical for ghetto operations, according to Brookings Institution economist James Sundquist. Aside from the unskilled labor problem, the scarcity of urban land along with its high cost, high taxes, high insurance rates, and difficult transportation, puts ghetto plants "at a marked competitive disadvantage."

Sundquist also concludes that prospects for "pure" black capitalism are even dimmer: "To suggest that Negro entrepreneurship can produce much more than a token number of new jobs for the hard-core unemployed, at least for a long time to come, is pure romanticism." The historical evidence seems to support this negative conclusion. At the turn of the century, Booker T. Washington campaigned for "black capitalism" and was strongly supported by the national corporate community, with the bulk of his financing coming from John D. Rockefeller, Andrew Mellon, Andrew Carnegie, and Julius Rosenwald. The dismal failure of the movement is evidenced by two surveys of black-owned companies, in 1898 and 1944, respectively. During this period of tremendous growth in American business, the average annual sales of these black firms actually dropped, from $4,600 to $3,300. At the end of the period the average black business employed less than four people, and was not strongly supported by the black community: for example, in 1939, black-owned food stores sold less than two dollars worth of food for each Negro in the United States.

The future of corporate efforts to overcome black poverty will partly be shaped by the fact that corporate action seems to move cyclically with the pattern of urban violence. As the years since 1967 have passed relatively peacefully, the fears of the danger have tended to fade, and with them the spur to action. Thus, the previously cited survey of top corporations' actions in the urban area notes that a new theme of "reflection" is partly explained by the fact that "after the two relatively 'cool' summers of 1968 and 1969, public and governmental pressure on corporations to act to ameliorate the urban crisis has somewhat diminished."

Corporate complacency is mirrored in the views of an important official of George Romney's Department of Housing and Urban Development, talking to the *Wall Street Journal*: "Environment, that's the thing to watch. That'll be the hot issue of the seventies. That's what the kids coming out of Harvard and Yale will be all charged up about. Urban matters will drop down." The fact that corporate ostriches cynically and shortsightedly bury their heads in the sand does not mean that the rising tide of black discontent will obligingly recede. It does, however, drive home that, while the problem of black poverty has at long last surfaced, it still appears to be insoluble within the sick society.

EPILOGUE: CHOCK FULL O'NUTS

CORPORATE BENEFICIARY OF OUR RACIAL SICKNESS

The activities of Chock Full O'Nuts Corporation, and its chairman, William Black, are a graphic illustration of the interrelationships of the problems besetting the sick society. It is also a revealing study of how individuals in this topsy-turvy society may produce antisocial results and yet be hailed as great benefactors.

To diners in eastern metropolitan areas where Chock Full O'Nuts has a string of modern luncheonettes, the company is probably best known for its tasty foods at low prices. For a wider radio audience Chock Full is the producer of "that heavenly coffee" about which a sexy female singer constantly serenaded millions of radio listeners. To the educational and philanthropic world it is the company founded and run by William Black, a leading donor for medical research.

These are the faces that Chock Full O'Nuts and William Black present to the world of white America. For the black community, however, whose view is from the underside, the picture is entirely different. First and foremost, Chock Full and William Black, who employ low-wage non-white labor almost exclusively, are major beneficiaries of the racial sickness that impoverishes black female labor.

The extent of the benefit is not revealed in any of Chock Full's annual reports, which give no data whatsoever on wages and salaries. Rather, it was accidentally exposed several years ago because of a thoughtless lark of some white college students. In the summer of 1963, at the height of the civil rights agitation, a handful of these insensitive young men picketed a Chock Full luncheonette on the grounds that the company discriminated *against whites* in its employment policy. In response Chock Full took out a full page ad in *The New York Times* to explain its position. In a letter signed by William Black, the ad first gave the company's view of why almost all of its employees were black:

Before the war, we were perfectly integrated. We hired high school graduates, and we paid no attention to the color of their skin.

During the war years, practically all of our white girls left. Because they were high school graduates, they were able to get office jobs.

The colored girls were also high school graduates, but they couldn't get office jobs—so they stayed.

The company then went on to assert that it was eager to hire white females, and listed the benefits its employees received, including the following: "We have been distributing 10% of our profits to our employees at Christmas. Last year it amounted to a half million dollars—over five weeks' salary for each employee." Now it takes only a little simple arithmetic to figure out that if 10 percent of the company's profits amount to over five weeks' salary for each employee, then the company's full annual profits equal about a year's salary for each employee! Thus, by its own admission, Chock Full made a dollar in profits for every dollar it paid its employees.

Thus, the foundation of Chock Full O'Nuts's success, and Mr. Black's personal fortune, derives from their success in employing low-paid black female labor. (At one point success was aided by constantly advertising that their food was "untouched by human hands," a theme that conveniently dovetailed with the racist fears of customers facing only black employees.) In turn, the company can get away with minimal wages largely because racial discrimination prevents Negro female high school graduates from getting higher paying jobs. (Moreover, bear in mind that until the late 1960s Chock Full did not allow tipping, which was presumably one of its appeals to thrifty customers.) The desperate economic situation of black women, which makes even a job at Chock Full seem attractive, is evidenced by the response to the company's 1963 ad specifically seeking more *white* employees. The company's employment offices were, according to Mr. Black himself, "swamped," but the overwhelming majority of applicants again were black. Of twenty white women accepted for employment, only three showed up for work.

Soon after these events Chock Full was picketed by six former black employees who had been trying to organize Chock Full workers into a union; these black workers were seriously protesting Chock Full's "de facto segregation" against whites. They were presumably motivated by a clear understanding of the link between racial discrimination that divides the labor force into warring groups and the lack of ability to organize unions under these conditions.

(It is interesting to note that the company apparently had long recognized its employee relations problems. In 1954 Jackie Robinson—the first black man ever to play in major league baseball, and a hero of the black community—was hired as vice-president for personnel, and in 1962 he was elevated to a directorship of the company.)

If this record of corporate profits from cheap black labor was the sum total of the story, it would simply be a dramatic version of an oft-told tale. However, there is more to the story because of William Black's particular role in society. His fortune made from Chock Full has enabled him to be a major donor to medical research, including $5 million for a twenty-story medical research building, $1 million for Lenox Hill Hospital, $1 million for Mt. Sinai Hospital, and $1 million for the Parkinson's Disease Foundation. Some of these gifts were the recipient organization's largest donation from a living donor (as opposed to a foundation).

One ironic aspect of Mr. Black's largess is that $5 million went to help build Columbia University's College of Physicians & Surgeons. Thus, Mr. Black's donation helped finance Columbia's expansion of its physical facilities, at a time when the black community was struggling to restrain Columbia from gobbling up yet more land:

> The plans to build an apartheid gymnasium set off the siege at Columbia University, but this scheme is a minor facet of the enormous realty consortia the university is forming with private industry. . . .
>
> Columbia dominates 15 other New York educational and medical institutions which cling together along the upper west side of Manhattan on Morningside Heights.

Thus, Columbia's continual encroachment on the real estate of the black ghetto, combined with the discrimination and poverty that prevents blacks from moving out, further worsens the plight of blacks.

It should also be noted that the hospitals to which Mr. Black is such a generous donor are major employers of black labor. Hospitals in the New York area have long established records of paying among the lowest wages of any industry, and hiring large numbers of blacks to do the lowest and most menial jobs. At the same time they have resisted attempts by these workers at union organization.

Interestingly, Mr. Black is adamantly opposed to any donations except for medical research, having refused to give twenty dollars to the Columbia Business School. He stated that "I wasted my time at the Columbia School of Business," because he did not think business could be taught. This is probably unfair to the Business School. Certainly no business school teaches prospective executives how to profit from racial discrimination, but surely the general ethics of corporate profit maximization are no barrier to capitalizing on such a situation. (As the Ford Motor Company slogan would put it, Black "had a better idea.") Again, Mr. Black has stated in an interview: "I hate waste; I squeeze the hell out of a tube of toothpaste," which sounds wonderful until one realizes that this concept of efficiency affects black women as well as toothpaste.

A final irony in the Chock Full story is that Mr. Black's profit-maximization drive has come home to haunt the citadel of the corporate society, Wall Street. A planned half-acre park within the financial district's canyons is to contain trees, shrubs, benches, and "an old, lopped-off building housing a Chock Full O' Nuts Coffee Shop." Why the eyesore? Because it is one of the three most profitable shops in Chock Full's chain, and Black refuses to vacate until his lease expires in 1980. An executive of a major Wall Street securities firm who wrote to Black threatening to organize a boycott, says, "I'm reacting as a public citizen who would like to see something pretty in a part of town that badly needs it." With the same cold logic that Wall Street uses in justifying investments in South Africa, Mr. Black has the irrefutable answer in the sick society: "We're not in business to give up stores. We are in business to grow. I wonder what the hell they would do if they had a profitable business and someone wanted them to give it up?"

To sum up, here is a case where a major corporation has built up large profits from black labor. It has benefited from the sick society's racism which creates a cheap supply of black labor, particularly female. From this corporation's profits, its founder has been able to be a major philanthropist, lauded for "his" generosity. His donations, the fruits of low-paid black labor, have come home to roost in the black community to further oppress it. Thus, black labor, through the medium of accumulated capital and the "generosity" of the owner of this capital, has come full circle to perpetuate the misery of blacks.

What is the moral of the Chock Full O'Nuts story? It is not, in my view, that individuals like William Black or institutions like Chock Full O'Nuts, Columbia University, or Lenox Hill Hospital are malevolent. William Black, in his role as chairman of Chock Full O' Nuts, is simply pursuing the normal corporate goal of profit maximization as best he can. William Black, in his role as philanthropist, is undoubtedly sincere in his efforts to promote medical research, just as the hospitals to which he donates large sums of money are unquestionably sincere in their efforts to better the conditions of their patients. Columbia University undoubtedly seeks to expand man's knowledge so as ultimately to promote human welfare.

Nevertheless, and this is the crucial point, in the sick society the road to hell *is* paved with good intentions. In the pursuit of their noble aims, each of these groups are forced by the total structure of the society to operate without regard to the ultimate consequences for large numbers of people.

5

ALIENATION

In recent years the existence of "alienation" has been widely recognized in the United States. "Alienated" has been a label attached to antiestablishment intellectuals, disaffected youths, and blacks. Thus, alienation is publicized as a phenomenon either outside of or on the periphery of the corporate economy. What I shall try to show, however, is that much of it is actually traceable directly to the workings of the corporate economy. Moreover, such alienation is, and is likely to be, a permanent feature of the sick society because it stems from necessities of the corporate economy, rather than from transient aberrations.

Black poverty, the U.S. expansionism which has culminated in the Vietnam War, and inadequately responsive political institutions, have all been widely observed as "causes" of alienation. I have previously analyzed these "causes" as intermediary "effects" of corporate dominated society. Now

135

I wish to go beyond these evident observations about alienation to examine other less publicized and fundamental aspects of this corporate-generated phenomenon.

Contemporary American alienation has two elements
that derive from negative feelings about the direct and
tangible operations of the corporate economy. The first is
the belief that the economy too frequently produces the
wrong things in terms of human welfare. It makes guns instead of butter, tail fins instead of schools, cigarettes instead
of cancer research programs. The second element is the
belief that the economy unfairly distributes the goods it
does produce. With the top 5 percent receiving four times
as much total income as the bottom 20 percent, extreme
poverty flourishes alongside of fantastic wealth. Moreover,
the inequities are not randomly distributed, but consistently
burden certain groups: blacks, Appalachian whites, the
aged, etc.

Other elements of alienation derive from negative feelings about the more intangible effects of the corporate economy. One is the feeling that this economy distorts human
lives and values. It is manifested in frequent complaints
about the "commercialization of life," "bureaucratization,"
"lack of community feeling." Another is the belief that, despite the existence of formal mechanisms of political democracy, our institutions are not responsive to the needs of the
people—somehow the "vested interests" will not allow us
to end horrible wars or terrible poverty.

A more subtle element of alienation is the feeling by
some corporate "insiders" that they are distorted by the
very corporate economy they help to run. This is probably
most keenly felt and expressed by those in the advertising
and entertainment industries, particularly the "creative
people." Its clearest manifestation is a widespread cynicism that can be seen as a protective device to shelter feel-

ings of having "sold out" skills and integrity in exchange for money. The extent of this feeling in the corporate community is much greater than the outsider might suspect. Many individuals, for their own peace of mind, have developed elaborate mechanisms to repress these feelings, an effort greatly encouraged by the corporation through its house journals, charitable drives, etc. If one cannot suppress these feelings, any expression of them, other than on a purely private and ineffectual basis, normally leads to quick expulsion from the corporate community. The result is that escape from the individual's psychic conflicts are most frequently sought in heavy drinking, frenetic activity to avoid thinking, and in more recent years, the suburban pot party.

Finally, there is an economic element of alienation that both cuts across and encompasses all the others. This is the realization of the enormous gap between the ideals of the economic system and its realities. Thus many people experience the sick society's increasingly glaring contradictions. How square the circle between the ideal of freedom and the reality of monopolistic restriction; between the ideal of truth and the reality of deliberate half-truths and outright lies; between the ideal of quality and the reality of engineered shoddiness; between the ideal of equity and the reality of rank discrimination?

Now that I have briefly described the set of beliefs, partially or totally subscribed to by "the alienated" in contemporary America, two critical questions need to be asked. First, are these beliefs more or less correct—i.e., are the alienated the healthy ones in the sick society, or the sick ones in a healthy society? Second, if the alienated are right, are these problems essentially accidental, and hence correctable within the existing order, or are they basic to the society and therefore insoluble within it?

From the title of this book my answer to the first question should be apparent. I will try to document my belief by providing examples of alienation culled from the vast body of data available.

I believe the economy produces the wrong kind of things in two different ways. It produces goods and services that are unquestionably absolutely harmful to people. Less obviously, perhaps, the economy also produces goods that are not intrinsically bad but are "wrong" because they require resources which could be used for fulfilling far more important human needs. The production of these latter goods—the vast panoply of luxuries—itself reflects the great inequality of income distribution within the sick society.

Foremost among the absolutely harmful products are the arsenal of military goods and services, ranging from hydrogen bombs to napalm to the training of young men to kill, which now costs the United States $80 billion per year. There is no point in belaboring this obvious item. Just how much the sick society's money drive has alienated its weapon users from other people is dramatically demonstrated by the contents of millions of "psychological warfare" leaflets rained down on North Vietnam in January 1967. These leaflets warned the North Vietnamese people that "their money would become worth less and less as the war went on." The extent to which the pursuit of profit has alienated the weapons makers from human values is strikingly illustrated in a letter to the editor of a radical weekly, signed by the president of the General Ordnance Equipment Corporation:

This correspondence is in reference to an item in your Dec. 16 issue headed "Cops use gas on Iowa Students."

We sincerely appreciate your mention of our products, but we wish to advise that "CHEMICAL MACE" and "MACE" are the Trademarks of General Ordnance Equipment Corporation, for its non-lethal weapons and liquid contained therein. . . .

You are undoubtedly aware that if our Trademarks, "CHEMICAL MACE" and "MACE" come into wide use as generic terms we might lose our Trademark rights to them, and we are sure you will want to assist us in preventing this.

In order to protect our rights, we would respectfully ask that whenever the terms "CHEMICAL MACE" or "MACE" are issued in any publication to describe our non-lethal weapons or the liquid projected by them, it should be placed in quotation marks, fully capitalized and accompanied by the symbol (R) which indicates that it is a Registered Trademark.

Also, if you wish to refer to this type of device by a generic name probably the best term would be "nonlethal weapon."

Such a letter, however, should not be surprising in a society whose widely sold consumer products are often lethal weapons.

Thus, the cigarette industry, despite abundant evidence that it contributes to thousands of deaths every year, strenuously resists any curbing. The kind of alienation generated within this industry and its supporters is eloquently indicated by an exchange between Emerson Foote, head of an advertising agency opposed to cigarette advertising, and a representative of the Agriculture Department, bastion of the tobacco interests. The Agriculture Department representative attacked Mr. Foote for failing to realize how crucial tobacco exports are for the U.S. balance of payments.

After a while, Emerson Foote answered:

"I guess I just don't think it's right to make a profit by killing people."

"Do you mean," the representative of the Agriculture Dept. replied, "that you don't believe in the profit system?"

Again, we have the drug industry, whose zeal to sell drugs good or bad—witness the Thalidomide scandal—has helped make it by far the most profitable industry in the country. U.S. Senate hearings on the drug industry have shown that the dramatic scandal is only the tip of the iceberg. For example, Parke, Davis & Company developed and had a monopoly on Chloromycetin, a drug appropriate for treating rare diseases like typhoid, which should be prescribed in only a few hundred cases in the United States. Yet according to Senator Nelson of Wisconsin, the company advertised it widely in medical journals without sufficient warning to doctors of its dangers, so that it was prescribed in 4 million cases a year! The rewards to the company in 1961 alone were its monopoly profits on total Chloromycetin sales of $59 million, less the relatively minor amounts paid out in damage suits prior to 1960 (the top one being $330,000 paid out to a woman who had the drug prescribed for a sore gum and developed aplastic anemia). The costs to society included about sixty needless deaths. Ironically, Parke, Davis's profits have plunged recently as its patent on Chloromycetin—its biggest moneymaker—expired and other large drug companies were also free to peddle the drug.

The callousness of the industry apparently even surprised a U.S. senator, who, from his lofty vantage point, has presumably seen almost every conceivable form of alienated behavior. Doctor Leslie Lueck, an employee of Parke, Davis was confronted by Senator Nelson with an ad for the drug in a British medical journal, containing no warnings of dangers. The doctor's defense was that the company always complies with any country's legal requirements for distributing drugs. This led to the following exchange, which incidentally pointed up the vulnerability of third world countries to U.S. corporate power:

"That sure shocks me," said the Senator. "What the witness says is, 'We will meet the standards of the country where the drug is sold.' That means of course there is not a single under-developed country in the world that has any defense against ex-ploitation of their people for profit by the American corporation which does not warn them of the serious, mighty serious, fatal, possibly, consequences here."

"You are indicting every drug company in Great Britain and the U.S.," replied Lueck.

"Any company that would do that, I would be pleased to indict," replied Nelson. "I think they ought to be indicted. Where the country is not protected, you tell us you have no compunc-tion about running an ad that will fool a doctor as you did in California. . . . I should think you people would not be able to sleep at night."

But sleep they do, as do the auto companies selling defec-tive cars, the chemical companies selling harmful pesti-cides, and all the other industries that have not yet met their Ralph Nader or Rachel Carson.

Somewhere between the absolutely harmful goods and the unnecessary luxuries turned out by the economy is an array of useful comforts that are produced but then artificially destroyed because they do not meet the profit-maximization needs of the corporate system. Vance Pack-ard's *The Waste Makers* has documented the innumerable ways in which companies engineer planned obsolescence into goods in order to increase their profits. I cite here only some of the more unusual cases. Potato peelers, which never wear out in normal use, have been "obsolesced" by paint-ing them the same color as potato peels, thereby assisting the housewife in accidentally throwing the peeler into the garbage with the peels. Similarly, the chucking out of usable drugs has been aided by the routine unwillingness of drug-gists to label fully their prescriptions. Finally, we may note the incredible efforts of the Holland Furnace Company, a company formerly listed on the New York Stock Exchange and the largest seller of replacement furnaces in the country. Company salesmen posed as government inspectors to gain entrance to a house, dismantled perfectly good furnaces, and then refused to reassemble them either on grounds of safety dangers or because the furnaces "were beyond economical repair"!

The unnecessary luxuries turned out by the corporate economy are legion. They range from the ridiculous— electrical cocktail stirrers and the like—to the sublime— the 100-room mansion built with the Dodge automobile fortune. At the extreme, the estimated 100,000 millionaires in the sick society (and particularly the few hundred worth at least $100 million) specialize in wasting society's resources not only through consumption of luxury goods but by wasting the lives of vast numbers of hired retainers. A *McCall's* magazine article on "The Care and Feeding of the Very Rich" reports on the behavior of Mrs. Robert Young, widow of the railroad tycoon, who likes trees: "She keeps her army of gardeners from boredom by having large areas planted, judged, found wanting, and dug up." There is clearly a similar labor-wasting component in the life of Mrs. Marjorie Post, who spends an estimated $2 million per year for "living expenses"! As the *McCall's* article notes, "Sleep-in masseurs, live-in golf pros, a come-in cook who can make lichee-nut omelets—those are the little things that make life so beautiful for the Beautiful People."

The primary basis for the production of relatively useless goods and services lies in the inequality of income distribution that permeates the U.S. economy. This inequality prevents a large part of the population from having the purchasing power to cause greater production of many of the necessities—let alone comforts—of life. At the same time, in recent years the stimulus to luxury production has been heightened by a failure of the sick society's much vaunted technology to generate *new* consumer products. While the early 1910s saw the rise of the automobile, the 1920s radio and refrigerators, the 1930s the washing machine, and the 1940s air conditioning and television, the 1950s and 1960s have produced nothing comparable to attract consumers. As a result, the strategy of marketeers focused on getting the more affluent consumers to buy two of everything, whether it be autos, homes or televisions, while at the same time trying to get them to buy bigger and more expensive versions of any given item. The pressure to get "forced consumption," as expressed by a marketing consultant in the mid-fifties, takes on overtones of a religious crusade, as indeed it must be for many corporations:

> Our enormously productive economy . . . demands that we make consumption our way of life, that we convert the buying and use of goods into rituals, that we seek our spiritual satisfactions, our ego satisfactions, in consumption. . . . We need things consumed, burned up, worn out, replaced, and discarded at an ever increasing rate.

The pressure for profits, in turn, leads to a wide variety of underhanded corporate behavior, ranging from the outright criminal to subterfuge, chicanery, and hypocrisy. The extent of criminal behavior by corporations was first laid bare in a classic study by an outstanding American sociologist, Professor Edwin H. Sutherland, in his *White Collar Crime*. He found from partial records that as of 1944 the top seventy industrial corporations had been held guilty of violations in almost 1,000 legal decisions;

these violations included restraint of trade, fraudulent ads, patent infringements, unfair labor practices, illegal rebates, etc. (Some of these decisions were in civil courts and before commissions, but even if this behavior were restricted to courts with explicit criminal jurisdiction, three-fifths of the corporations had been convicted at least once.) Ninety percent of the corporations had been caught at least four times, which as Sutherland notes, in many states would cause an individual to be designated as a "habitual criminal." This sordid public record existed despite the fact that hushing up of corporate crimes is widespread. Finally, as Ferdinand Lundberg has shown, this pattern of corporate crime exists to this day.

It is worth pointing out that these corporate crimes are no trivial matter, but vastly exceed in total cost to society all the violent street crimes against property that the mass media feature daily. For example, it is estimated that in 1968 the total value of property stolen from individuals was less than $55 million, while business frauds alone robbed individuals of over $1 billion. If jail sentences were meted out to corporate executives with the same severity as those given ordinary criminals who steal large sums of money, many executive suites would be swept clean for years to come. (Big electrical equipment manufacturers, drug makers, and concrete pipe producers—to name a few recent corporate criminals—have agreed to reimburse hundreds of millions of dollars stolen through price fixing.)

Finally, there is a vast range of business activity that strictly speaking is not illegal, but even in the eyes of the practitioners is highly unethical. Many books have documented this at length for the advertising business; this industry's very existence is based primarily on making a mountain out of a molehill, or even a mole. But, every industry has its own tricks, which together add up to a horror story for the public. For the reader who is interested in the gory details I recommend the "Naders Raiders" reports, Vance Packard's works, or the many business novels, especially those written by people who have quit industry. I cannot refrain from quoting, however, the experience of one of Sutherland's young acquaintances who presents his own deflowerings by various industries with the innocence of the Marquis de Sade's *Justine*:

When I graduated from college I had plenty of ideals of honesty, fair play, and cooperation which I had acquired at home, in school, and from literature. My first job after graduation was selling typewriters. During the first day I learned that these machines were not sold at a uniform price but that a person who haggled and waited could get a machine at about half the list price. I felt that this was unfair to the customer who paid the list price. The other salesmen laughed at me and could not understand my silly attitude. They told me to forget the things I had learned in school, and that you couldn't earn a pile of money by being strictly honest. When I replied that money wasn't everything they mocked at me: "Oh! No? Well, it helps." I had ideals and I resigned.

My next job was selling sewing machines. I was informed that one machine, which cost the company $18, was to be sold for $40 and another machine, which cost the company $19, was to be sold for $70, and that I was to sell the de luxe model whenever possible in preference to the cheaper model, and was given a list of the reasons why it was a better buy. When I told the sales manager that the business was dishonest and that I was quitting right then, he looked at me as if he thought I was crazy and said angrily: "There's not a cleaner business in the country.". . .

Then I got an opportunity in the used-car business. I learned that this business had more tricks for fleecing customers than either of those I had tried previously. Cars with cracked cylinders, with half the teeth missing from the fly wheel, with everything wrong, were sold as "guaranteed." When the customer returned and demanded his guarantee, he had to sue to get it and very few went to that trouble and expense: the boss said you could depend on human nature. If hot cars could be taken in and sold safely, the boss did not hesitate.

The corporate world takes for granted the widespread existence of these unethical practices and only divides as to whether business has the right to use them if they are legal. On the one hand, a writer in the *Oil and Gas Journal* seems to take pride in that industry's long history of questionable practices:

Ever since a railroad conductor named Drake drilled that first oil well under the phony title of "colonel," oilmen have been engaging in a socially accepted and mutually enjoyed game of deceiving each other. Drillers do their best to pull the wool over each other's eyes, and competitors resort to ingenious devices to find out what's going on. . . .

Industrial espionage is as old as competition and there may be a fine legal line between its commendable and reprehensible forms. But the oil business has made an honorable profession out of spying.

On the other hand, a recent *Harvard Business Review* article arguing that deception is necessary for success in business brought forth a varied reaction from its corporate readers. Some said this was an atypical view, while others claimed that "sound ethics is good business." Interestingly, one businessman wrote that after reading this article he realized his customers must be cheating him, and that from then on he planned to cheat with all the rest! From my experience, the weight of evidence is on the side of the view of the anonymous businessman who said, "A sudden submission to Christian ethics by businessmen would bring about the greatest economic upheaval in history."

The virtually inevitable result of an economic system that produces too many wrong things, distributes even the right things unfairly, and resorts to widespread subterfuge in the process, must be basic distortions of human beings on an epidemic scale. The corrupting process starts with those who ride the tiger—corporate management. Vance Packard's *The Pyramid Climbers* shows how management personnel themselves are viewed and treated by the corporation as commodities, just like ordinary labor (albeit scarcer). Thus, management is recruited, developed, graded, and stockpiled in the same way pigs and chickens are processed under modern agribusiness; for example, there is frequent overt reference within the large corporation to its "inventory" of managers. In this process, individual managers are continually being evaluated and compared for their potential to move up the corporate ladder, with the primary criterion naturally being the individual's contribution to profit growth.

Given this enormous pressure, it is hardly surprising that the picture which emerges of the corporate executive is, in human terms, little short of ghastly. To take an example, we have the word of the head of a leading executive employment agency that one out of every twelve executive job seekers lies about his educational background by giving himself a nonexistent degree. A Stanford psychologist's study of personality types in different occupations finds that corporate sales managers generally verge on the maniacal. Finally, a psychiatrist who has worked with many corporate executives hands down an even more general indictment of the sick society's top leaders: "Most executives truly know very little about one of the most important things in life—the true meaning of love in its broadest sense."

It may be argued that the corporation does not generate personality distortions among its managers, but simply attracts a certain type of person in the first place. Certainly there is evidence to support this selection theory. Thus, studies of college graduates show that those who enter business are strongly motivated by "leadership" and "money," while they rank very low in originality and creativity or willingness to help others. It might be noted that even if this theory were wholly correct, it would hardly be cause for cheer that the country's major institutions have such a perverse selection mechanism.

However, it seems eminently clear that the behavior patterns which any personality type is forced into in his functioning within the corporation undoubtedly serve to change his initial personality for the worse. Take as an illustration our young "Justine," as he describes his reaction to finding out that the used car business also was crooked:

When I learned these things I did not quit as I had previously. I sometimes felt disgusted and wanted to quit, but I argued that I did not have much chance to find a legitimate firm. I knew that the game was rotten but it had to be played—the law of the jungle and that sort of thing.

Vance Packard, who affirms his faith in the corporation, concludes: "the aspiring executive's system of values tends to go dangerously askew when he is expected, as increasingly he is, to make a total commitment to the promotion of goods or services that are frivolous, of dubious social value, or perhaps even harmful."

The alienation generated by the corporate system is not

limited to management but extends down through the labor force and into society as a whole. As C. Wright Mills noted, "When white-collar people get jobs, they sell not only their time and energy but their personalities as well." This, according to a sales manager of a large corporation, requires them to be willing to use "every conceivable dirty trick" because: "The constant everyday pressure from top management to obtain profitable business, unwritten but well understood, is the phrase 'at any cost.'" The corroding results on the salesman's personality are described with wonder by our sadder-but-wiser Justine of the used car business:

The thing that struck me as strange was that all these people were proud of their ability to fleece customers. They boasted of their crookedness and were admired by their friends and enemies in proportion to their ability to get away with a crooked deal: it was called shrewdness. . . . It was just good business.

Once in a while, as the years have passed, I have thought of myself as I was in college—idealistic, honest, and thoughtful of others—and have been momentarily ashamed of myself. Before long such memories became less and less frequent and it became difficult to distinguish me from my fellows.

Just as the salesman manipulates his customers in the sick society, he in turn is manipulated by his superiors, who are aided by alienated scientists. Thus, a psychologist working for a management consulting firm notes the problem of the salesman who "feels he has earned enough to satisfy his financial needs" (God forbid) and therefore "no longer pushes himself" (death of the system, let alone the salesman!). His suggested solution: offer noncash prizes appealing to the salesman's family that will pressure him to work harder. Says the psychologist, "Never underestimate the power of a woman and the family in planning a sales contest," in advocating this modern corporate version of divide and conquer.

Alienation of the blue-collar labor force, stemming from the same corporate drive for profit maximization, is also widespread. The workers' response to the ever present pressures for labor cost reduction—whether they take the form of speed-up with old methods or "automation"—may vary from bitter resignation to bitter industrial sabotage. What is well-nigh universal is the absence of any pride or joy in the highly specialized and intensely repetitive labor process. Instead, workers live for their paychecks and the things they can buy with them, which in turn makes them easier prey for the dream merchants of corporate advertising.

Moreover, the blue-collar worker is constantly subject to alienation generated by the drive for profit maximization. To take a particularly blatant example, in the emotion filled atmosphere prevailing at the time of the killing of Martin Luther King, many businesses closed on the day of his funeral. According to the *Wall Street Journal*, a survey by the Philadelphia Chamber of Commerce showed that about one hundred Philadelphia companies allowed employees time off to view the funeral on television, but while salaried employees were paid, hourly employees were not!

Starting from the center of the production and distribution process, the blight of alienation then spreads naturally to the political sphere. Earlier I analyzed the institutional mechanisms by which the corporate economy holds sway over much of the political apparatus. Here I wish to point up the frequent personal and human alienation that is an inevitable by-product of this relationship.

On the one hand, corporations demonstrate daily by their deeds that profit is their overriding goal, and that monopolistic restriction, subterfuge, and manipulation of labor and consumer alike are working tools toward this end. On the other hand, public office holders, be they President, congressman, or judge, are sworn to defend and advance the highest ideals of the society—freedom, honesty, and justice. But, since the corporate economy is highly successful in screening out from political leadership those who would "rock the boat" by attempting to bring corporate reality into line with these ideals, those who attain public office normally are "worldly wise." Is it any wonder that all too often they are either cynics or amoral predators whose behavior ranges from the unethical to the clearly corrupt?

An extreme example of the absence of moral values is reported by an able journalist:

Not long ago, a newspaper editor chided a wealthy and powerful United States Senator about activities of his that seemed to be misuse of public power for private gain. The editor expected a flat denial or some kind of rationalization. He was completely taken aback when the Senator said bluntly that of course he had used his position to add to his multimillion-dollar fortune.

"What do you think I spent all that money getting elected for if I didn't expect to get more back?" the Senator is quoted as saying.

Arrogance about unethical behavior is epitomized by a pillar of the Establishment, the late Senator Everett Dirksen, whose law clients included International Harvester Company, Pabst Brewing Company, the National Lock Company, and Panhandle Eastern Pipeline. During a Senate debate on proposed legislation to insulate federal regulatory agencies from political pressures, Dirksen proclaimed that he would continue pressuring these agencies on behalf of his "constituents" as long as the law did not say he could be "put in jail for doing it."

Charges of ethical inconsistency in the U.S. Senate as a whole were made by one who is in a good position to know, U.S. Senator Russell Long. In the course of defending Senator Dodd on corruption charges, Long stated that half the members of the Senate Ethics Committee "couldn't stand the investigation Senator Dodd went through" and that "half the Senate" was equally guilty.

Corruption may be even more widespread at lower legislative levels. In the words of former U.S. Senator Joseph Clark:

It is the third branch of government, the legislative, where things have gone awry. Whether we look at city councils, the state legislatures or the Congress of the United States. . . This is the area where democratic government is breaking down. This is where the vested-interest lobbies tend to run riot, where conflict of interest is concealed from the public. . . .

As a recent illustration, we have the case of Paul Powell, secretary of state in Illinois, who labored for thirty years as a member and leader of the state house of representatives. While his total income for his public service, his only occupation, was less than $300 thousand, he left an estate valued at about $3 million, including $750 thousand in cash hidden in his closet. Says one former colleague, "I sure was surprised at how much Paul left—I thought he'd leave a hell of a lot more." In the words of the *Wall Street Journal*, the Powell case is "a textbook illustration of close links between state legislators and the special interests they are supposed to regulate."

On occasion, even the country's most sacred institution, the presidency, has not been safe from profit-driven individuals—witness the case of Warren G. Harding. Lyndon Baines Johnson, *during* his presidential term, not only failed to sell his extensive holdings in the government-regulated radio-television industry, but added substantially to his property holdings. According to *The New York Times,* at various times he purchased through agents many acres of Texas land—purchases soon followed by new state highway and bridge projects which ultimately would greatly enhance the land values. (Ferdinand Lundberg reports that this "led Washington wits to say that Mr. Johnson has been the biggest real estate operator as President of the United States since President Jefferson's 'Louisiana Purchase' "; the remark itself indicates the extent of Washington cynicism about the moral standards of public officials.) Considering that Johnson built himself a $10-20 million fortune largely through his powerful congressional position, his record is eloquent testimony both to the money drive generated by the sick society and its moral corruption.

Finally, the distortion of human values generated by the corporate system spreads into once relatively untouched areas of culture. As James Ridgeway notes in his study of "American Universities in Crisis," "Professors once sneered at businessmen and the profit motive, but since they have been so successful in taking up the game themselves, the profit motive is now approvingly referred to as the 'reward structure.' " (Whereas the management consulting firm I once worked for used deliberately, but approvingly, to call the profit motive "greed" so as to get its business clients to face reality more effectively!)

At the extreme, learned scientists and leading educational institutions profitably use their skills to develop monstrous weapons of chemical and bacteriological warfare; the aim is to be in a position once again to loose the plague upon mankind. Learned social scientists, with university and foundation support, also provide major theoretical underpinnings and practical applied knowledge for everything from suppressing revolutions to assisting motivational researchers in conning consumers into buying products. How far along the road of alienation social science has traveled in becoming a tool for marketing (let alone death) in this way is stated clearly by an advertising executive, writing under a pseudonym:

Social scientists in the past have paid attention to the irrational patterns of human behavior because they wish to locate their social origins and thus be able to suggest changes that would result in more rational conduct. They now study irrationality—and other aspects of human behavior—to gather data that may be used by salesmen to manipulate consumers.

The most pervasive and important cultural institution of the sick society is the "wasteland" of television. Despite its enormous potential, television—virtually from its inception—has been simply a corporate enterprise renting the use of the airwaves to other large corporations who use any kind of "entertainment" to help sell on a mass basis. As a corollary, "quality" programs which cannot help sell on a mass basis, or are presumed unable to do so, normally cannot be seen on television. In the words of a spokesman for television writers, defending their failure to write plots accurately portraying black people (a failure that further contributes to the sick society's endemic racism):

Content in TV is, and has always been, under the direct control of the corporations who pay the bills: the networks, the advertising agencies and sponsors. All of us, the writers, the producers, the independent packagers, are employees of these companies. Essentially we write to order. We think to order.

Or, as a forthright television producer, who thinks that logically the advertising agencies should produce the television shows, stated it:

> TV viewers cannot be regarded as an audience to be entertained. . . . *They are prospects . . . for what the sponsor has to sell.* This fact constitutes the show's reason for being. . . . Thus in a TV production the selling motive stands as the dominant factor.

The observant reader may note the striking similarity between this last view of the audience as "prospects to be sold" and that of the ghetto merchant who sees his customers as animals to be trapped. This should not be surprising, for the economic base of the sellers is the same in both cases: namely, monopolistic control that prevents the potential customer from having any real choice.

Everyone in the sick society suffers to some extent from the alienation of the individual as a deliberately manipulated consumer. Some aspects of the manipulation are indeed bizarre, such as the long-term campaign of hair preparation manufacturers to convince white women that wavy hair is the best, and black women that straight hair is the best. While this may appear trivial, it is typical of the many corroding attempts at inducing in all Americans insecurities to be fixed by consumption. Listen to the words of the chairman of one of the country's largest corporations, Allied Stores:

> Basic utility cannot be the foundation of a prosperous apparel industry. . . . We must accelerate obsolescence. . . . It is our job to make women unhappy with what they have. . . . We

must make them so unhappy that their husbands can find no happiness or peace in their excessive savings.

But, what is the effect on the human personality of living in a society which, according to an official of General Foods, exposes the typical family to 1,518 selling messages a day? What can be the quality of life when genuine emotions become simply vehicles for the big corporations— when a major department store fills its windows on Valentine's Day with mink stoles and negligees and a sign asking "How do I love thee? Let me count the ways?"; or when druggists all over the country are told Valentine's Day is "a real sweetheart of a day . . . to cash sentimentality into dollars"; or where one of man's greatest achievements, his flights to space, are quickly converted to profit seeking: "Apollo 7 medics recommended antihistamine and decongestant for astronaut's cold," advertises the makers of Dristan tablets.

Is it surprising that in this environment Americans of all classes feel restless and unfulfilled, and that, on average, U.S. families, regardless of their incomes, wish they earned 25 percent more than they actually do? Or, that a substantial number of Americans do not believe we ever landed a man on the moon, including many who saw the moonwalk on television but believe it was faked? Or, that a young black concert pianist and Yale-trained musicologist, unable to make a sufficient living as a music teacher, joins an advertising agency, explaining quite accurately:

Music is the servant of the society in which it happens to find its life. . . .

If I was born 300 years ago I'd be working in a church in Vienna and on the outside writing music for Saturday night gigs.

In our society, though, the forms of musical expression that are rewarded by the society are the ones that deal with the major aims of the society—that's selling.

Perhaps the most tragic aspect of the corporate-spawned alienation is its drive toward self-perpetuation through gaining control of the minds of the youngest children. Television has provided the ideal mechanism for turning our children into what David Riesman has aptly characterized as "consumer trainees." The corporate dream has been all too clearly spelled out by one professor pointing out the advantages of "investing" in child conditioning:

It takes time, yes, but if you expect to be in business for any length of time, think of what it can mean to your firm in profits if you can condition a million or ten million children who will grow up into adults trained to buy your product as soldiers are trained to advance when they hear the trigger words "forward march."

Is this, then, the inevitable future shape of life in the sick society? Or, are the aspects of alienation discussed here "accidental" attributes of the corporate system, and amenable to reform, as the liberal vision would have it? My view is that the specific elements of alienation in the sick society may change, but the total configuration cannot and will not; liberal reformers have gotten cigarette advertising driven off radio and television, but hydra-headed it will just increase in newspapers, magazines, and the omnipresent outdoor billboards. For it is the roots that determine the fruits, and the economic causes of alienation are not accidental attributes but intrinsic elements of the corporate society.

Thus, the system must produce the wrong goods precisely because, as its supporters claim, it produces according to the impersonal and unbiased "dictates of the market." In practice this means production according to the real or corporate-engineered "needs" of those who have money. Who has money, in turn, is largely determined by history: the rich own the corporations that give them further wealth, while the poor have only their meager skills that yield them poverty wages or unemployment. Given the gross inequalities of starting point, the iron law of the market "unbiasedly" and "impersonally" dictates the inevitable results—e.g., that a wealthy man's whim for a million dollar country home must take precedence in commanding lumber and carpenters over the needs of a hundred slum families for minimal decent housing.

Similarly, the market mechanisms of the corporate society insure that mass culture will be a shoddy product, and where it is not, it will be largely unattainable by the poor. Thus, the central aim of every corporation, large or small, is somehow to keep prices above what they would have been with competition. This requires monopoly control, and if necessary, creation of artificial scarcity. Since the price that television corporations can charge (directly to the advertiser, but ultimately to the mass consumer) is determined by the size of their audience, they aim at the lowest denominator to maximize their audience and profits; their virtual monopoly control insures that those for whom they have hit too low will also come along, lacking any real entertainment alternatives.

At the other extreme, commercial theaters and sports stadiums, which due to technology cannot have nationwide audiences, usually aim at low volume and high prices. Only in a market economy do we take as "normal" the coexistence of half-empty stadiums and sports-loving children idling on slum streets, or unemployed concert musicians and elderly music lovers both sitting dejectedly at home.

But, what is to be expected from a society which finds it "cheaper" to pay blacks welfare pittances rather than harness their energies at decent wages to clean up and rebuild the ghettos?

The unequal distribution of wealth and income, which is the starting point of our problems, has not, New Deal, Fair Deal, New Frontier, and Great Society notwithstanding, changed significantly over the last twenty-five years. Thus, Herman Miller, a leading government expert on the problem noted in 1964 that "a myth has been created in the United States that incomes are gradually becoming more evenly distributed. . . . There has been no appreciable change in income shares for nearly twenty years."

Moreover, the sick society's governments are not likely to change this situation in the future, because a redistribution of income shares is hardly likely to be demanded by the power-wielding upper class. In most societies it is not only the use value of wealth that is important to its owners, but also its relative scarcity. Particularly in a materially oriented society, where the ownership and control of money is the most fundamental mark of social status, it is crucial that these major inequalities continue to exist.

In response to this "need," the sick society has developed strong mechanisms to insure that inequality remains. At the economic level, the high tax on current income contrasted with the zero tax on wealth, plus the existence of the corporation as a vehicle for transforming current income into lightly taxed additional wealth, insures that the wealthy will continue to maintain their favored economic position.

In addition, the close relationship between wealth and political power vitiates the potential threat to economic inequality always inherent in universal suffrage. The fact is that the basic requirement today for obtaining political power is the ability to command other men's labor and skills, whether it be to print a poster, write a speech, appear on television, or buy some favors. As *Business Week* somewhat cynically put it, "Money is only one ingredient in a candidate's campaign kit, but it is far ahead of whatever is second." In this struggle for command of resources, $10 million held by one man has far more power than the same amount held by a thousand men with $10 thousand apiece. The thousand, even if highly motivated, can spare only a small part of their money for political purposes; the wealthy individual can spare most of his without in any way impinging upon his luxury living. The recent rash of politically obscure millionaires who have launched themselves as senatorial or gubernatorial candidates attests to the increasing capitalization on this situation.

Finally, it is inherent that the system must distort values in the direction of acquisition-mindedness, because mass consumption is crucial to its viability. Thus, advertising *is,* as its defenders claim, a necessary component of the U.S. economy. It is particularly important today because capital expenditures by consumers—for housing, automobiles, and appliances—now approximate in size business capital expenditures, traditionally the backbone of the economy. Since this consumer capital spending is by its nature deferrable, the unceasing efforts of advertising are required to induce consumers to keep these purchases on a high and ever rising level.

Nevertheless, despite the valiant efforts of the hucksters, income inequality itself is an insoluble threat to the stability of the economic system. This income inequality makes it impossible over the long run to match consumption with potential production. Why? Because the wealthy receive, directly or indirectly, enormous incomes that they cannot spend. Even after allowing for unmatched levels of luxury living, the rich collectively have enormous sums available for investment, which they undertake indirectly through the medium of their ownership of the major corporations. But, as the corporations accrue greater and greater wealth, and plow back the accumulated profits into further investment, they run up against the barrier of finding markets for their ever increasing productive capacity. In recent years this barrier has been pushed back by American overseas expansionism as well as by providing increasing credit to the lower and middle classes to purchase more goods than their current incomes and even savings will allow. However, as I shall show in Part III, overseas expansion and consumer credit have limits beyond which the economy cannot go without ultimately initiating a major monetary breakdown. In point of fact, these limits have already been passed.

In the final analysis, then, I believe there is no hope for elimination of widespread alienation from the sick society. This does not mean, however, that we are doomed to suffer eternally. Rather, in my view what is doomed is the sick society itself. Why this is so, and what will replace it are the key questions of our time. It is to these questions that the remainder of this book is addressed.

PART III

THE IMMEDIATE
CRISES

PROLOGUE

We have previously examined some of the major ills of the sick society—ills that may be viewed humanistically as symptomatic of its fundamental rottenness. However, these diseases have existed for decades, and if they were the only ones afflicting the sick society it could probably continue on its present path for generations to come. What makes this highly unlikely is that two less widely recognized crises are developing which are even more dangerous to the system's health because they threaten its very existence. These attacks on the lifeblood of the sick society—its money—are the focus of this section.

First, there is its international illness, as evidenced by the recurrent gold and dollar crises. Second, there is the internal fever, as evidenced by rapid inflation and the enormous rise of personal and business debt. These crises are interrelated, and are likely to lead to a major monetary breakdown that will badly damage, if not destroy, the very sinews of the sick society. Moreover, for reasons I will indicate, the monetary illnesses are so advanced and of such a nature that it is highly unlikely that Dr. Government, even armed with a full load of Keynesian medicine, can save the patient.

6

THE INTERNATIONAL
MONETARY CRISIS

Within the last few years the capitalist world has been
rocked by a series of monetary crises, including the British
pound devaluation, a run on the dollar, and most recently,
a bitter struggle between the mark and the franc. That
these events have not merely signaled esoteric problems of
technical financial adjustments can be deduced from the
behavior of the western world's financial and political
leaders at the November 1968 monetary conferences. According to *The New York Times*:

[A senior] Bonn official described an oral message transmitted
by Prime Minister Wilson of Britain to the [German] Federal
Government on Tuesday as "uncouth" in its language and political threats. The official also said that Roy Jenkins, Chancellor
of the Exchequer, had been "ill-bred" in remarks to Finance
Minister Franz Josef Straus. . . . An official German source
described Mr. Fowler's [United States Treasury Secretary] conduct at the conference as "impudent."

At the core of these recurring monetary crises is the struggle over the role of gold versus the U.S. dollar in the world economy. Underlying this struggle in turn, in my view, is a fierce economic and political power struggle between Western Europe (and Japan) and the United States over the role of American investment in these countries. The mechanics of the struggle are such that its resolution may be determined in the end not by officials of nations involved, but by individual speculators on both sides of the Atlantic, with potentially disastrous consequences for all.

In order to understand the nature and significance of the present international monetary crisis, some historical perspective is needed. In the 1930s, as a result of the Great Depression and the specter of war, capital fled from Europe to the United States, which built up an enormous gold hoard. This stock of gold rose from $10 billion in 1935 to $22 billion in 1940, at which time the United States held the bulk of the world's gold. World War II physically destroyed the economies of all the European powers but Great Britain, which it vastly weakened. At the same time, the economic and financial power of the United States was greatly increased; its gold holdings reached a peak of $25 billion in 1949.

The Marshall Plan helped to rebuild Europe, but partly, as we have seen, at the price of increasing U.S. penetration of Europe and former European colonies. The book value (basically the original cost) of direct U.S. foreign private investment rose worldwide from $12 billion in 1950—the order of magnitude at which U.S. overseas investment stood in the 1930s—to $33 billion in 1960, and to about $75 billion today. And everyone agrees that these figures greatly understate the real value of the assets the United States has accumulated. (As an example, the whole of U.S. Middle

Eastern oil investment is carried on the books at $1.5 billion, but this figure excludes the value of the 150 billion barrels of oil proven to be in the ground; that is one reason the reported rate of return on Middle East investment is more than 50 percent per year.) Thus, what these figures really show is not the absolute level of investment, but its rapid rate of growth.

At the same time, in almost every year since 1950, the United States has had a balance of payments deficit. This means that, including our foreign investment overseas, we have spent more abroad than foreigners have spent here. How have we paid for this deficit? The answer, of course, is to be found in the historic willingness of foreigners to accept dollars or gold in exchange for giving the United States real economic assets. Until 1957 foreigners were willing to take dollars, and the U.S. gold hoard stayed at about the 1950 level. From 1958 on, however, foreigners began increasingly to demand gold, and the U.S. gold stock has shrunk to about $11 billion.

Why the shift? One reason is that, despite current U.S. assertions to the contrary, gold is still the only universally accepted currency. The ultimate strength of the dollar as an international currency lay in the huge supply of gold available to reclaim any unwanted dollars presented at the U.S. bank window. As the supply of dollars in the hands of foreigners grew increasingly larger than the value of U.S. holdings in gold, the creditors naturally became increasingly suspicious of our ability to pay their claims in the only currency they really trusted.

A second reason was the drive, particularly by the French under de Gaulle, to slow down U.S. investment in Europe. This investment has risen from $2 billion in 1950 to $6 billion in 1960 and to about $25 billion today. The theory was that if Europe demanded gold, the United States would have to curb its dollar outflow in order to maintain its gold stock, and ultimately would have to cut its foreign investment. Put another way, as long as Europe was willing to pile up dollars, the United States could go on building and buying real assets in Europe (as elsewhere in the world).

The French foreign trade secretary, on visiting the United States, presented the position as follows:

We could permit a much larger American presence in our economy as the Germans are doing, and it would be easy politically. There would be more jobs and faster growth. But to be politically responsible to the generations to come, we have to see that these generations have the weapons to defend themselves— economic weapons. If we did nothing, in a few years we would have the same problems as Latin America has. The idea has taken hold in American financial circles that the way to take care of the United States' favorable balance of trade with France is to export capital. This is a policy whereby we could become a medium developed country in the future. This explains our attitude on gold. *We don't want to take America's gold, we just want to stop the overabundance of American capital in France.*

The United States, on the other hand, has strenuously resisted these efforts to curb its overseas investment. The entire history of the government's programs for reducing our balance of payments deficit—from the first attempts to decrease loans to foreigners down to the pressure on American corporations to borrow abroad—shows the desire to find other solutions, short of seriously constraining the growth of U.S. foreign investment.

On a theoretical plane it has sometimes been argued that there is nothing inherently wrong with the deficit. This view was well stated by three leading U.S. economists,

Emile Despres, Charles Kindleberger, and Walter Salant, writing in the London *Economist* (which dubbed their position "the new nationalism"):

The dollar is the world's standard of value. . . .
An annual growth in Europe's dollar-holdings averaging, perhaps, $1½ to $2 billion a year or perhaps more for a long time is normal expansion for *a bank the size of the United States with a fast-growing world as its body of customers.*

Now, if this struggle were merely between the United States and France (or between the United States and a de Gaulle obsessed with power, as it was sometimes portrayed), then it would have only fleeting historical interest, thanks to U.S. far greater power. But it seems clear that de Gaulle's position had, and continues to have, strong if quiet support in continental Europe. In the money arena, actions speak louder than words. Back in the late 1950s most of the continental governments held little gold. Today, while France holds about $3.5 billion worth of the metal, West Germany has $4 billion, the Benelux countries over $3.5 billion, Italy $3 billion, and Switzerland $2.5 billion. Thus the Common Market countries and Switzerland together hold over $15 billion in gold, which accounts for two-thirds of their international reserves. Lest one think that this merely reflects nervousness on the part of all foreign governments as to the redeemability of the dollar, note that for the rest of the world, excluding the Common Market countries, Switzerland, and the United States, the proportion of gold to total reserves is only one-third. The United States's best customer on the basis of holding dollars is Japan, which keeps less than one-seventh of its reserves in gold. Japan, however, restricts American investment by more direct means, ranging from outright prohibition of foreign investment in some industries to requiring joint venture investments in others.

To sum up, in the last decade the increasingly dominant factor in U.S.-European economic relations has been the growth of U.S. foreign investment. This growth has been, in my view, the basic cause of the dollar outflow which, as these dollars are cashed for gold, has led to the gold crisis in the United States. Where do we go from here? The situation is now critical and something must give.

To see what is likely to give one has to examine the balance between two basic sets of economic forces. The first set is the real economic forces, involving the control of production and profits. The second set is the financial forces, involving control of money and gold.

As to the real forces, the most important fact of current international economy is the enormous United States position overseas. The view from Europe on this situation has been dramatically summarized in *The American Challenge* by Jean-Jacques Servan-Schreiber: "Fifteen years from now it is quite possible that the world's third greatest industrial power, just after the United States and Russia, will not be Europe, but *American industry in Europe.*" This is true despite the fact that less than 10 percent of European industry is now controlled by American corporations. While still relatively small, this investment is growing much more rapidly than the indigenous investment. Also, U.S. investment is heavily concentrated in the key growth industries—computers, electronics, chemicals, etc. These are not only the high-profit industries but also the high-technology industries that all agree will dominate the future economy.

Moreover, the simple arithmetic of foreign investment must also disturb Europeans: with U.S. investment in

Europe earning 10 percent per year, while the European economies grow at perhaps 5 percent per year, the United States could steadily increase its share of industry in Europe merely by plowing back profits made in Europe. Using European labor and European markets, American industry could grow toward domination of Europe without sending an additional dollar from the United States.

For the same reasons—high profits plus great growth potential—U.S. industry has a strong interest in increasing its European investment. In addition, American industry wants a heavy investment in Europe in order to profit from its investment in raw material production in the underdeveloped world. For example, there would be far less value in the enormous U.S. oil investments in the Middle East and Africa if that oil could not be pumped into European refineries or marketed to European customers, as is now done on such a huge scale.

While many Europeans have pointed out the dangers of U.S. domination of their industry, they face for several reasons an apparent dilemma in dealing with it. For one thing, the separate European nations are too small consistently to generate companies as large and powerful as those that have grown up in the vast U.S. market and are now invading Europe. Size provides major advantages, not only by allowing low-cost mass production but also by providing the huge resources needed to invest in new developments, particularly those of technology, in training management and in other intangibles. (Thus U.S. international companies have benefited most from the European Common Market because since its inception they have organized operations to compete in the whole market rather than in single countries.)

Another problem for those who would curb the

Americans is the disunity of the Common Market countries. The fact is, as de Gaulle learned several years ago, that if France says, "No, we will not allow a U.S. auto firm to put a plant in France," the company can outflank him by building it in a neighboring country (in this case, Belgium) and exporting to France.

A more fundamental problem is that if the Common Market countries adopted a united front to constrain further U.S. investment, but took no other steps, they would fall further and further behind technologically (where technology includes not only the fruits of research and development, heavily subsidized by the U.S. government, but also managerial and organizational improvements). But "machine breaking" will work no better now than it ever has in the past, and one way or another Europe will "acquire" the new technology. If U.S. firms cannot bring it in outright through investment, they will "smuggle" it in by embodying it in U.S. exports. Thus the new technology incorporated in cheaper and superior U.S. goods would not only capture markets in Europe but also in the rest of the world and thereby render impotent a European economy heavily dependent on trade. Rather than suffer this catastrophe most Europeans would probably choose direct U.S. investment. The end of that road might be a psychically painful Canada-type satellite economy with the bulk of industry owned by the United States, but at least the standard of living would be relatively high.

The solution that most Europeans would obviously prefer is for Europe "somehow" to create its own resources for overcoming the "technology gap." The major snag is the investment, enormous relative to Europe's resources, required not only for building new factories but also for research, education, etc. For example, the French government had to allocate $80 million as an initial sum merely for research, to launch an all-French computer company which it was hoped would be a viable competitor to the U.S. giants.

If money is the main obstacle, one key to obtaining resources for European self-development may lie in Europe's vast gold hoards. In a sense, what is needed is a reversal of the basic exchange that has underlain U.S.-European economic relations for two decades. During this period the United States has built up enormous real economic power in Europe by investing in factories and business organizations. In exchange, Europeans have accrued enormous financial power in the form of hoards of gold and dollars. Up to this point it has been a poor trade for the Europeans because the gold and dollar hoards are essentially sterile; the gold earns nothing and the dollars, even when held in U.S. Treasury notes, earn only a small percentage a year. U.S. foreign investment, on the other hand, is far more profitable and can grow rapidly simply by profit plowback. Moreover, while the purchasing power of the dollar declines in the current inflationary period, the value of the U.S. investment rises.

The Europeans cannot catch up now simply by disgorging their gold and dollar hoards, because this would encourage the United States to accelerate its investment. After all, it is only the Europeans' increased appetite for gold that has forced the United States to make any attempt to slow down its overseas investment program. But Europe now has an opportunity to attempt to recoup some of its losses through a worldwide devaluation of the dollar along with all other currencies, i.e., by a big jump in the price of gold.

A worldwide devaluation of all currencies by the same percentage would not change their exchange relationships: one U.S. dollar would still equal 3.7 German marks or 5.6 French francs. Hence no country would gain a trade advantage over any other. The primary beneficiaries would be the major gold-producing countries —South Africa and the Soviet Union—plus countries with large hoards of gold, that is, most of continental Europe. The Common Market countries alone hold close to $15 billion in gold officially, and private accumulations tucked away in mattresses and Swiss safe deposit boxes may be on the order of $10 billion. Thus, if the price of gold was doubled, the Common Market countries would enjoy a "windfall profit" on the order of $25 billion, or about the book value of U.S. investment in all of Europe.

Such an enormous windfall could go a long way toward making Europe a great independent industrial power. Some of it might be used to buy out at premium prices the European plants of U.S. firms, or even in certain key industries to purchase the complete operations of smaller U.S. firms with good technological prospects. More important, most of this money could be spent to improve education, support basic and applied research, and promote European firms in the crucial growth sectors. Such efforts would be greatly assisted by the fact that the bulk of the windfall would accrue directly to the European central governments. While the governments could either set up state (or even interstate) companies, or liberally subsidize private firms in the crucial industries, the fundamental point is that the money would be initially concentrated where presumably there would be a will to use it.

The United States government is completely opposed

to such a worldwide devaluation. To see one obvious reason, imagine a poker game with two players, Sam and Charlie. They start off the game with 20 poker chips each which they agree to value at $1 apiece. Midway in the game Charlie, who has had a run of good hands, finds himself with 30 chips while Sam has 10. Charlie then says, "This game is so much fun that I think we ought to raise the value of these chips to $2 each." Normally, Sam's reply would be unprintable, since under the new rules he would be losing $20 instead of $10. (The increased loss as a result of the change in the rules is a function of the difference between the two players' piles of chips.) If we substitute the United States for Sam, Western Europe for Charlie, gold for poker chips and a 50 percent currency devaluation, i.e., a doubling in the price of gold, for Charlie's suggested rule change, then we have a good first approximation of the tensions now underlying the international monetary system. (Interestingly, William McChesney Martin, Jr., the former chairman of the Federal Reserve Board, recently admitted that in the late 1940s "some of us" thought the price of gold should be raised because the United States had the largest gold stock and would benefit the most.)

Still, it is conceivable that the European governments could force the issue, either by threatening to "bankrupt" the United States by demanding gold in exchange for their dollars, or by concertedly devaluing their own currencies and thus threatening the U.S. trade position. One may well ask why, if a jump in the price of gold would be so enormously profitable for the Europeans, they have not taken either of these steps toward a devaluation in their currencies.

One major deterrent is the fear that any massive change

in the value of currencies could so shatter confidence in international finance and money markets as to wreck international trade and bring on a world depression. Thus, *Business Week,* in analyzing the dangers of a foreign central bank run on the U.S. gold supply, reports:

"Anyone starting an avalanche," says a U.S. official, "would have to be afraid that the avalanche would catch them, too." A European banker agrees. "Whatever fears we have about the dollar," he says, "they aren't enough for us to want to destroy the system."

An additional danger is that even if Europe were united on this strategy it would probably provoke an open and violent struggle with the United States. The United States has a tremendous stake in not letting Europe simply buy out investment that has been built up over twenty years, or in allowing Europe to develop the kind of rival economic base that would threaten the profits of U.S. firms.

One weapon the Americans might use, and one which they have hinted at, is the countering of a European run on their gold supply by refusing to have anything further to do with gold. According to these quarters, the value of Europe's gold hoards might then shrink drastically since only the willingness of the U.S. government to buy and sell gold at thirty-five dollars an ounce keeps the price that high. Lacking that support, it is said, the price of gold would sink toward its market value as an industrial metal, estimated by some at less than ten dollars an ounce. While Europeans may doubt the ability of the United States to abandon gold, as well as the consequent drop in price if it did, the situation is sufficiently uncertain to signal caution. For one thing, U.S. abandonment of a fixed gold price would mean freely fluctuating exchange rates, and could lead to a division of the world into separate gold and dollar trading blocs. This in turn might prove a serious barrier to international trade.

All parties agree that something must be done soon about the precarious situation. The United States sees a long-run solution in the ultimate elimination of the role of gold (and implicitly the triumph of the role of the dollar) in the world monetary system. In fact, U.S. monetary experts sometimes talk about the gold problem as if it were caused by a psychological hang-up on the part of those who so tenaciously cling to the yellow metal; William McChesney Martin, Jr., of the Federal Reserve Board even referred to it in recent years as a "barbarous relic." Were it not for the fact that the United States takes this position primarily because of its own difficulty in holding on to gold, this might be construed as a truly radical statement for a leading capitalist official. For if gold is a barbarous relic, then so too may be the whole capitalist system, because gold is the purest form of money, and money is the lifeblood of the capitalist system.

As for the technology gap, the U.S. position seems to be that Europe is foolish to worry, since U.S. control of European industry will bring with it a rising standard of living. But if Europeans insist upon indigenous control of industry, then a "United States of Europe" should be formed with Great Britain as a key component. In practice the aim of the United States is to soft-pedal the problem, recognizing that time is on our side; increasing U.S. investment in Europe will eventually reduce the latter to Canada's status, which is perilously close to a fifty-first State.

The European response varies within and among countries, depending largely on particular self-interests.

But there is certainly general agreement among Europeans, who for two decades have provided the United States with billions of dollars worth of factories in exchange for millions of ounces of gold, that now is no time to "forget about" this barbarous relic just because it has little "intrinsic" value. (By analogy, the rest of the world might tell the United States to forget about its overseas factories and mines, since its claim to them rests in ownership certificates that are just worthless pieces of paper that cannot even be used to fill teeth; such is the subversive logic of those who would consign gold to the monetary scrap heap.) Europeans must find this U.S. attempt to downgrade gold particularly irritating because twenty-five years ago at the Bretton Woods Conference the United States rejected Keynes's proposal for an analogue of the current "paper gold" plan precisely because we insisted on the supremacy of metallic gold. At that time of course, the United States held two-thirds of the world's supply.

As to the immediate financial crises, Europeans also generally agree that the U.S. balance of payments deficit must be reduced as a first step. One reason for this agreement is the widespread belief that inflation is being "exported" from the United States to Europe, as the flood of dollars is exchanged by Europeans for their own currencies, thereby generating inflationary tendencies. It now seems clear that at the historic Basel meetings of March 1968, where the two-tier gold price system was established and agreement was reached on the creation of special drawing rights ("paper gold"), this agreement was coupled with an understanding that at a minimum the United States would seek to reduce inflationary pressures. One way *not* to achieve this would be to escalate the war in Vietnam. The *Wall Street Journal* quoted an expert commenting on the abdication of Lyndon Johnson immediately following the March gold crisis:

The European financiers are forcing peace on us. For the first time in American history, our European creditors have forced the resignation of an American president.

But how much additional pressure the European governments would be willing to exert today is not at all clear. The crucial question would seem to be whether European capital is really prepared to slug it out with U.S. capital for supremacy in Europe, and ultimately for a significant position in the underdeveloped world, or whether it is prepared to accept the subordinate role of running the relatively stagnant and less profitable traditional industries such as textiles and steel. Given the rate at which technology is developing, a decision must be made before the U.S. lead becomes virtually insurmountable.

Undoubtedly there are strong groups within Europe that would be content with a subordinate position. For example, the Belgian steel producer who can have his profits improved by computerization may be eager for IBM to come in with the best equipment available. Again, European executives of U.S. firms, or the indigenous suppliers of these firms, may be eager for further U.S. expansion.

Nevertheless, in my view the Common Market countries have not yet reached the point where their capitalist class as a whole is so weak as to be unwilling to fight for these new markets. Many competent European companies are holding their own in the face of fierce U.S. competition. Moreover, a wave of European mergers is developing that can help strengthen their financial ability to move into the new industries. Thus, if the European governments felt they had a reasonable chance to effect the kind of financial coup discussed earlier, they would probably ultimately make the attempt.

In the last few years, however, the financial crisis has so accelerated that the final resolution may no longer lie in the relatively cool and carefully calculating hands of European and U.S. governments, but rather in the hot and irresponsibly greedy hands of the world's monetary speculators, including the world's largest international corporations. Unlike our previous analogy, the game is far more complicated than one between Sam and Charlie. There are perhaps a dozen important official players—the United States, the important gold-holding governments of Western Europe, Japan, the big gold producers like South Africa and the Soviet Union—and thousands of unofficial players. The latter get into the game by speculating in the international money markets on the relative values of different currencies and gold.

Thus, international finance has become the world's most widespread crap game, with potential quick profits that make the rewards from speculation in "cats and dogs" on the American Stock Exchange look feeble by comparison. Bets are usually placed either by selling short on a specific weak currency that might have to be devalued (and can thereby be bought back later at a lower price) or by buying gold in the hope of a universal currency devaluation.

The first case that whetted the appetites of the world's "hot money" gamblers was the successful 1967 raid on the British pound, which ended in devaluation. This was not only enormously profitable to the speculators but also showed such speculation to be a favorite sport for a much greater number of people than ever before. A *Wall Street Journal* report neatly captures the flavor of the game:

Some of the boys in Youngstown, Ohio, found the stock market too erratic for their taste last week, so they looked for something safer—like a raid on the British pound sterling.

The group—eight to 10 doctors, lawyers, and other professional men with a sophisticated bent for speculation—made their decision Friday to plunge into the murky waters of international finance. By 2 P.M. (E.S.T.) when the time difference cut short their trading, they had borrowed and sold short 70,000 pounds.

"We thought we'd have time to sell more pounds short Monday," says one of the group, but Britain's abrupt devaluation Saturday night ended the foray. Selling short 70,000 pounds is small compared to operations of bigger speculators and bear raiders in Continental Europe. But it was enough, with the devaluation, to assure the Ohioans collectively a profit of more than $23,000 on the $20,000 cash they put up to go short on sterling valued Friday at nearly $196,000.

The second round of speculation centered on private purchases of gold in the open market, which in 1968 drove the price of gold up to forty-five dollars an ounce. Furthermore, it forced the United States and European governments to close down their international gold pool, which had previously successfully stabilized gold at thirty-five dollars an ounce. While gold's price declined below the forty dollar level, speculators who had bought at the official support prices of thirty-five dollars and sold at forty dollars realized a few hundred percent profit on their investment in a short time (most of the money to buy gold is borrowed from banks on margin, thereby "leveraging" the speculator's own money). The third round of speculation in 1969 also led to high profits from the devaluation of the franc as well as the revaluation of the German mark.

The very activities of monetary speculators can help to make the rumors of world wide devaluation a self-fulfilling prophecy. For one thing, the difference between the free market price and the official price of gold is often a naked index of world confidence in paper moneys. As the gap—which is itself stimulated by speculative buying —gets wider, foreign central banks may begin to panic and turn in their dollars to Washington for gold; in some cases they may be tempted even to resell this gold secretly on the private market, at perhaps fifty dollars per ounce, and then seek more gold from the United States at thirty-five dollars per ounce. As an economist connected with a European government put it, "There are a lot of crooks around, and some of them are central bankers." The net result could be to force a worldwide devaluation, but it is also possible that the international monetary system might break down.

Finally, in a period of increasing monetary uncertainty, speculators jump on any currency that looks weak, and sell it short. The resulting further weakening frequently is vastly accelerated by the "hedging" of large corporations seeking to protect themselves from a possible currency devaluation; this hedging can take various forms, but all of them have a similar effect as speculative short-selling. Since this is a game where he who stumbles gets kicked again to keep him down, such speculative pressures can themselves be the deathblow. Any devaluation now of a major currency could force a self-protective chain reaction ending in universal devaluation.

I stress here the profit-seeking aspects of the international monetary problems because to me this is the frequently overlooked key. As always in capitalism the name of the game is money, and on the international monetary scene the players are either big capitalists—individuals or large corporations—or governments trying to protect and further the interests of their own capitalist economies. It is important to keep this in mind because so often the public discussion of international financial problems takes place on a lofty and abstract plane. The causes and cures of the problems are seen to lie in technical difficulties and their adjustments (or sometimes in the "irrationality" of certain leaders, e.g., de Gaulle). It is as if profit, as well as the power that goes with profit, were farthest from the minds of the participants in the monetary problems. (The extent to which participation in the monetary arena allows an aura of sanctity and high moral purpose as opposed to being for one's own specific gain can be seen from the following general situation. Only in the money field are the ideas of company officials [bankers], about what should be the price of the commodity they sell [interest rates], taken as if they were disinterestedly for the general good. A steel company official who made such a claim about steel prices would be laughed off the floor.)

The impractical textbook nature of most of the proposed solutions to the international monetary crises is one reason that these solutions have little chance of being adopted, let alone of succeeding. With the capitalist world fundamentally fragmented and with real economic and political power at stake, any change in the monetary rules that favor one party will normally hurt another. In the arena of international finance today the principles of military strategy are operative. Thus, "reform" schemes, which assume that power is a commodity that can be increased absolutely and divided equitably, leaving a neat balance, are likely to fail. This is particularly true when they assume a world of consensus rather than the real world of conflict.

One "reform" that many people appear to believe would alleviate the international monetary crisis is for the United States to reduce its overseas military commitments, especially by getting out of Vietnam. While there is no question that these commitments have contributed heavily to the U.S. balance of payments deficit, it is unlikely that they have been or will be decisive. For one thing, this military posture has been a bulwark for the massive U.S. investment in the underdeveloped countries, the profits from which greatly reduce the deficit. More immediately, most American foreign aid, including military aid, is tied to purchases of U.S. goods. Moreover, the United States had balance of payments deficits for many years before Vietnam became a major drain. Finally, there is no sign of any immediate end to this war, and, even if peace broke out overnight, the prospects of some reduction in the U.S. balance of payments deficit would seem insufficient to resolve the world monetary problems; foreigners already have far more dollars than they really want.

To conclude, the recent monetary crises should have made clear that underneath the veneer of cooperation that glosses the international monetary system, the law of the jungle still operates. The post-World War II system worked well as long as the United States was the solitary lion and could enforce stability with its undisputed power. Now that European "tabbies" have grown into (nonpaper) tigers and are contesting both the United States and each other for a place in the sun, the situation has become inherently unstable. This instability is then worsened by the wolfpack speculators, who leap collectively at the throat of the first currency that threatens to lose its footing in the struggle.

Thus, whether the latest bout of speculation leads to immediate currency changes or the Vietnam War is ended is less important than the fact that the prospects for orderly reform of the international monetary system appear extremely dim. According to an International Monetary Fund expert, "For all practical purposes it would be impossible to put through an orderly realignment" of major currency relationships. If this be so, given the underlying conflicts of U.S. and European interests in the international economy, the upshot of all this wild speculation could turn out to be a chaotic rout for all. Financial markets could collapse, international trade and investment dry up, and internal economies be badly depressed. To assess the grave consequences for the sick society, we have first to examine its own internal economic ills; these too are quietly but rapidly building to a critical stage.

7

THE DOMESTIC
ECONOMIC CRISIS

In recent years economists of all political persuasions have tended to deprecate the threat of cyclical instability in the U.S. economy. The Keynesian theory of the New Economics, apparently "proved" by the relatively steady growth of the U.S. economy since World War II, has almost silenced the skeptics and seems to promise that a major economic depression is now impossible. However, the fabled power of government to prevent any such major downturn in the present U.S. economy is at best untested and I believe will prove to be in practice nonexistent.

The basic danger to the U.S. economy is one that is always present in a capitalist economy—the possibility that monetary conditions will get out of line with physical production and consumption needs. In my view, a crucial source of potential imbalance results from the tremen-

dous post-World War II growth of credit that has helped
fuel the real economic growth in production and consumption.

In a sense, the last twenty-five years have witnessed a
new development of capitalism, what one might call
"credit capitalism." Earlier, the most important developments in capitalism were in the area of production (assembly lines and mass manufacturing), and somewhat
more recently in the area of marketing (advertising, mass
distribution, etc.). Today the emphasis in the business
world is increasingly on the selling of credit. While sales
on credit are not new, what is new is both the scale and
the fact that, as Hillel Black notes: "Credit has become
an end in itself. In many instances more profit is derived
from credit than from the goods and services being sold."

"Credit capitalism" is really the highest and purest
form of capitalism. For one thing, nothing tangible is
produced, so that there are few labor problems; com-
puterized records are substituted instead. Second, credit
capitalism has the potential of being automatically self-
perpetuating, in that interest on the debt continually
adds to the amount of debt outstanding. The ultimate
success lies in getting a person so addicted to credit that
he borrows more money simply to pay off his old debt.
As a small loan company businessman stated to Mr. Black:

> The key to our success, and that of any loan company, is to
> increase our loans outstanding. As soon as the account is about
> to liquidate, we take immediate steps to renew the loan up to
> $500, the maximum allowed in this state. One of the things we
> do is to find out if the customer has other debts. Then we call
> him up and offer to consolidate them. Our best customers, I
> might add, are the old timers. At least we know their habits.
> The idea is quite simple. Prevent the customer from getting off
> the hook.

A consequence of this shift toward "credit capitalism" is that the economy becomes increasingly "illiquid." This has been happening here in the postwar period, and as a result our economy is increasingly vulnerable to the danger that a small downturn will develop into a major crisis. I shall try to show why it is unlikely that the government could contain the spread of a crisis based on this fundamental financial weakness.

In saying that the economy has become increasingly "illiquid" I mean the following. At any given moment there exists an amount of legally fixed obligations (debt repayment plus interest payments) that must be met. The supply of money that exists to meet these obligations consists of cash and currency in circulation, plus the checking accounts (demand deposits) at commercial banks. (In practice, checking accounts ultimately created by bank loans to businesses comprise the bulk of this money supply.) On top of this monetary base is a superstructure of various "liquid assets" that can more or less readily be converted into money to meet the obligations, either by selling them on the open market (corporate stock) or by demanding cash for them (savings deposits).

The economy tends to become less liquid when one or more of the following occur: the ratio of money to debt falls; the ratio of money to liquid assets falls; within the liquid asset superstructure, the proportion that can more easily be liquidated falls.

What distinguishes a "less liquidable asset" from a "more liquidable asset"? In answering this question, it is essential to recognize that while for an individual or firm a particular liquid asset may be viewed as equivalent to cash, it may not prove so if many individuals or firms try to convert it at the same time. Thus, it is liquidity as an objective social factor rather than as a subjective individual phenomenon with which we are concerned. Viewed in this light, liquidity may be defined as the extent to which relatively simultaneous attempts by large numbers of individuals or businesses to turn the particular asset into money could be effectively realized. This in turn partly hinges on the extent to which a mass attempt to exchange a particular asset for cash could be facilitated by the government without serious negative consequences for the economy.

Finally, a real danger point is reached when the ratio of debt to money is so high that debtors, seeking to obtain new loans to make interest payments or to refinance their old debt, help drive interest rates to very high levels. "Tight money" and high interest rates tend to slow real economic activity by curtailing home construction, business investment, and state and local governmental borrowing and spending capability. Concurrently they also tend to cause a slide in the stock market, partly as a result of investors selling stocks in order to buy high-yielding bonds. This in turn may put further downward pressure on real economic activity because serious declines in the stock market can trigger a shriveling of business and consumer confidence that leads to reduced production and spending plans. This, in turn, leads to greater unemployment, further lowering of income and purchases, even greater unemployment, and so on.

To see how real is the danger of such a monetary crackup, one must examine the postwar changes in the liquidity position of various sectors of the economy, because the liquid position of one group does not offset the illiquid position of another. Thus, if one looked simply at gross changes in the liquidity picture for the economy as a whole in the postwar period, one could be reasonably optimistic. In 1945, total financial assets for all sectors of the economy were $800 billion, while total financial liabilities were $650 billion, leaving net assets of $150 billion, or less than one-fourth of liabilities. By the end of 1968 total financial assets of all sectors had quadrupled to $3,810 billion, while total financial liabilities had increased only to $2,820 billion, leaving net assets of $990 billion, or one-third of all liabilities.

These figures, however, mask an ominous decline in the real liquidity position of certain sectors of the economy during the same period. Particularly following the Penn Central Railroad bankruptcy, the squeeze on corporate treasuries has been widely discussed. (Corporate holdings of cash and government securities as a proportion of their current liabilities had dropped from 73 percent in 1946 to 19 percent in 1969.) Less publicized is the drop in household liquidity. Thus, the net worth of individuals has increased four-fold since 1945, but in that year 14 percent of all household financial assets were in currency and demand deposits, and another 19 percent were in U.S. government securities; in other words, one-third of individual assets were highly liquid. By 1968 the proportion of individual assets held in these highly liquid forms had declined to only 11 percent. On the other hand, back in 1945 corporate stock accounted for only 30 percent of all household assets. By 1968, corporate stock made up 47 percent of household assets.

These changes in the composition of assets are particularly significant because of the growth pattern of household liabilities. The two most important components, mortgages and consumer credit, have increased almost twenty-fold since World War II, with the total household mortgage debt amounting to $260 billion at the end of 1968, and consumer credit standing at $110 billion. (Bank loans and other liabilities increased eight-fold to $55 billion in 1968.)

There is no doubt that this tremendous upsurge in individual borrowing has been a significant factor in the postwar growth of the economy. For present purposes, however, the point to note is that the kind of individual debt which has increased most rapidly has been the one usually incurred by the lower and middle classes. The big increase in individual assets, on the other hand, has come in holdings of corporate stock, which have risen from $110 billion in 1945 to $870 billion in 1968, and are owned overwhelmingly by the top 1 percent income class.

To fully appreciate the real social and economic dynamite embodied in this debt-asset split, we need to look more closely at exactly who are the debtors and who are the stock owners.

The most striking aspect of the debt picture is that consumer installment credit is already a major burden on the poor and the working class. More than 10 percent of the families who earn under $7,500 per year (45 percent of the entire population) have to devote more than 20 percent of their income to debt repayment; only about 5 percent of middle-income families ($7,500 to $15,000 income) have a similar debt burden, and only 2 percent of the upper-income group (over $15,000) must worry about debt repayment. Even worse, among the most debt-ridden families—those who use more than 40 percent of their income for debt repayment—the majority have incomes under $3,000 per year.

We do not have any detailed breakdown of debt by race. One available figure, however, is quite revealing:

while 46 percent of all white families have some amount of installment debt, the comparable figure for blacks is 64 percent. Moreover, the average amount owed by blacks ($970) is three-fourths of the white average, despite the fact that the average income of blacks is only about three-fifths that of whites. Since over 80 percent of all black families earn less than $7,500, it is clear they are a key part of the working class and the poor who are most heavily burdened by debt.

Similarly, debt is a greater burden for young families than for older ones. Seventy percent of all families whose head is under thirty-five years of age have some amount of installment debt, compared to only 30 percent of families whose head is over thirty-five. The families that are most burdened by debt, however, are those whose head is under twenty-five, for over 20 percent of these families need one-fifth or more of their annual incomes for debt repayment.

By contrast to this installment debt, home mortgage debt is much more a problem of the middle class. The under $7,500 income group accounts for only 20 percent of all mortgage debt, while the $7,500-$15,000 class bears 60 percent of it. This is not surprising because one normally needs a fairly high income in order to get a mortgage and to be able to meet the mortgage payments. Nevertheless, for the 15 percent of all families earning under $3,000 per year who do have a mortgage, about 25 percent of their income goes toward interest and amortization payments on this debt.

The distribution of stock ownership by income groups, on the other hand, is diametrically opposite. While about one-fourth of all families own some stocks, stock ownership occurs among only 12 percent of those in the lower-income groups, 30 percent in the middle class, and almost 60 percent in the upper class. Moreover, the value of stocks owned by low-income families averages around $1,000, while almost two-fifths of the families in the upper income group own stocks worth at least $5,000.

Three things stand out from these debt and asset data. First, installment debt (which is the most expensive type of debt, usually costing about 18 percent per year), is a particularly great burden on the poor and the working class, especially blacks and young people. Second, home mortgage debt is primarily a burden on the middle-income group. Third, ownership of the most important form of assets, corporate stock, is overwhelmingly in the hands of the upper-income group. One major implication is that in the event of a significant economic downturn, since the groups that are most burdened by installment debt would be those who have the least job seniority, namely, blacks and young people, the capacity for this type of debt to be repaid would rest upon the weakest link in the economy. Second, if the downturn continued further, the viability of mortgage debt would be dependent upon the group that would be second hardest hit by a recession, namely, the middle class. The upper-income group's vast holdings of corporate stock would be of little support to the debt structure in recession, because the upper-income group has relatively little debt.

Finally, the political and social implications of this situation, which we shall return to later, are enormous precisely because blacks and young people are the groups most alienated from the sick society. Hence, it is highly unlikely that given a major economic downturn, which would make many of them bankrupt and destitute, these groups would be willing as their parents did to patiently wait for the kind of relief the New Deal fumbled toward in the 1930s. Rather, their response to such a situation would likely be to demand radical action fast, thereby bringing them into open conflict with the inertia that is fundamental to the political structure of our society. Such a conflict could lead to a social explosion.

As for the possibilities of a major economic downturn getting started, they have paradoxically been increased by the prosperity of the last twenty-five years. For one thing, steady economic growth, by increasing individual incomes and hence borrowing power, has permitted the great increases in household debt, but in effect this debt borrows from potential economic growth in the future.

More immediately, the enormous growth of mortgage debt has led to potentially great financial and credit instability. M. Carter McFarland of the Federal Housing Administration has charted in detail the declining quality of residential mortgage debt in the postwar period. When the FHA was established in 1934, the maximum loan-to-market value ratio for a mortgage was 80 percent; by 1950 the actual ratio for new single family homes had increased to 88 percent and by 1964 it was nearly 95 percent. At the same time, the maximum repayment period has been extended from twenty to twenty-five years in the 1930s, and up to thirty-five years today. (FHA government-insured loans have decreased from about one-quarter of all residential loans in the thirties, and 45 percent during the war, to only 13 percent in 1964.) Summing up, McFarland notes that these trends represent:

. . . a rather revolutionary departure from the time-honored lending theory that the soundness of mortgage lending is directly related to the extent to which the value of the mortgaged property exceeds the amount of the mortgage debt. . . . *High ratio mortgage lending, particularly without government insurance, represents an act of faith in the stability of the economy, in relatively full employment, and in the stability of real estate values.*

These mortgage trends are particularly dangerous because the banking and financial system itself has become increasingly illiquid, with the great growth in its relatively illiquid assets coming precisely in the area of mortgage debt. In 1945 all banking institutions had deposit liabilities (excluding those of governments) of $110 billion, against which their holdings of mortgages equaled $14 billion, or only 13 percent. By 1968 the deposit liabilities had quadrupled, but bank holdings of mortgages had increased eighteen times, to $250 billion, or more than 50 percent of deposits. As a corollary, the ratio of banks' liquid assets (defined here as cash and U.S. government securities) to deposits of individuals and corporations has dropped sharply, from 126 percent in 1945 to 36 percent in 1968. The savings and loan associations, which were created to provide mortgage money, are the country's fastest growing banking institution (total assets increasing from under $10 billion in 1945 to $150 billion in 1968) and are naturally the most dependent upon mortgage debt; it accounts for 85 percent of their total assets.

Thus, mortgages are a focal point for the destabilizing forces within the economy. On the one hand, interest and principal repayments on home mortgage debt, which at present amount to perhaps $25 billion per year, are an important claim on the earnings of millions of lower- and middle-income families. On the other hand, the banking system has become heavily dependent upon these mortgages as their ultimate security for deposits. Meanwhile, the quality of mortgage debt, as traditionally measured, has seriously deteriorated.

Thus far the structure has not broken down, and the most important reason, probably, is the continuous price inflation since World War II. From the home owner's point of view, general inflation has the great virtue of making it easier to meet fixed interest and debt payments. While for the same reason general inflation is undesirable from the mortgage lender's viewpoint, inflation in the real estate market is a comfort to him because, if the borrower defaults, he will not lose out. Thus, McFarland has this to say about the period of rapid inflation in housing right after World War II:

Indeed, in such a market it was difficult for any party to the transaction to make a mistake. Mistakes in judgment on the purchaser's part were quickly covered up by the rapid inflation of the price of his house. If he ran into personal difficulties, lost his job or was transferred out of town, he could usually bail out of the mortgage obligation he had undertaken and frequently do so at a profit. The heavy insulation provided by rapidly rising values and the ready saleability of properties also protected the lender against the normal hazards of mortgage lending, and against mistakes he may have made in appraising the property or the borrower.

If inflation has been a crucial element in maintaining past financial stability, then prospects for the future are indeed horrendous. The sick society now is hung up on the horns of a fatal dilemma: intolerable inflation versus intolerable depression. As we have seen, the ending of inflation is necessary, although not sufficient, to prevent an international monetary breakdown; just how much longer Europeans will be willing to accept the decline in the value of their dollar holdings owing to U.S. inflation is anyone's guess. Equally important, there are tremendous internal pressures for action to prevent inflation from getting out of hand, before it leads to the historical reaction of a great crash.

One problem is that the tremendous past growth of inflation and debt are accompanied by, and also engender, expectations of ever increasing economic prosperity. Individuals borrow freely, blithely assuming that their future incomes are sufficiently secure to meet increased obligations. Lenders, bathed in the same euphoria, cut corners and lend to virtually all comers. Exuberant expectations lead to exuberant activities that fuel inflation and produce further exuberant expectations and an increasing speculative atmosphere. In the process normal standards of economic calculation fall by the wayside. Thus it is perhaps not surprising that until the 1969 bear market, numerous investment funds sought only a "moderate" 50 percent appreciation of capital in eighteen months. Similarly, real estate companies in California "realistically" looked forward to appreciations in land prices of 35 percent a year.

Even more important, the behavior of the largest corporations in recent years has become increasingly speculative, and based on the same expectations of continued inflation. For one thing, corporations are reinvesting their profits as quickly as possible, before costs rise in the future. For example, a late 1969 *Wall Street Journal* story headlined "The Land Rush: Corporations Grab Up Sites for Expansion and for Speculation," pointed out that corporate executives were not worried about the high land prices because they assumed they will be even higher in the future. Again, until the 1970 recession many corporations were "stockpiling" labor, in order to be sure that they had enough to increase production in the presumed inflationary boom period. Similarly a significant part of the very high rate of business investment in plant and equipment which resulted in an increasing gap between capacity and current production must represent speculative stockpiling of physical facilities.

The corollary of this is that as each business frantically flees from money into goods, it makes itself increasingly illiquid. Thus, General Electric Company today has about the same cash balances that it held in 1946, even though its sales have grown tremendously; for all manufacturing corporations together, while sales have doubled in the past ten years to $165 billion, cash and marketable securities have stayed at the same level of about $30 billion. How this is accomplished by some major corporations is indicated in *Business Week*: "An Eastern electronics company staggers payments to creditors according to how loud they squawk; a Midwest conglomerate writes checks on Fridays and hopes it has enough cash coming in on Monday or Tuesday to cover them; a major diversified consumer products company frequently has to borrow from the bank to pay its current operating expenses."

Perhaps most dangerous of all, the commercial banks, the backbone of the monetary system, similarly threw caution to the wind in their activities. For one thing, these banks are trustees for vast pools of capital, and in an attempt to stem the outflow of these funds to the then highly successful "go-go" mutual funds, they sought to improve their own investment performance by increasing speculation in the stock market. At the same time, with the enormous demand for loans, business and personal, the banks reduced their own liquidity to levels that would never have been tolerated in a more rational period. More conservative banks frequently were dragged into the performance race, since failure to take the risks that all other banks were taking would make the conservative bank less profitable, at least in the short run. And, it is this short run that is characteristically of the greatest concern in a speculative period. After all, whether it be investment in chain letters or Dutch tulips at $10,000 each, who worries about the underlying reality when there is always a sucker to whom you can sell them at a higher price? Only when growing numbers of people begin to see that the emperor may in fact be naked do reality considerations, followed by panic, begin to intrude.

Exactly what specific form such a money crisis economic breakdown would take in our society is virtually impossible to know in advance. But to illustrate the mechanics of such a process, as well as the monetary interrelatedness of all sectors of the economy, one hypothetical but plausible set of events is presented below. It should be stressed that this artificially constructed model is not a forecast of *specific* future events.

As a result of the international maneuverings over the balance of payments crisis, involving various currency devaluations, international trade and investment slows down. Because of this, U.S. exports begin to weaken, thereby slowing production at home. At the same time, as a result of the international monetary pressure to reduce U.S. inflation, military spending is reduced.

The cutback (or even a slowed growth) in military spending hits southern California particularly hard because it is a major defense supplier. Some people are laid off, but more important, the exuberant expectations about the area's growth, which had been fueled by the rapid increase of military expenditure, are suddenly cooled. The real estate and mortgage market in southern

California rapidly begins to deteriorate. One or two major western savings and loan associations are unable to meet new withdrawals by nervous eastern depositors. They are taken over by the Federal Home Loan Bank Board, which begins to liquidate their mortgage portfolios.

Savings and loan depositors all over the country begin to panic, and to demand their money. As a result of this rush all depositors cannot be paid off promptly and must wait. Clauses allowing the savings and loan associations to defer immediate payment are invoked on a mass basis. This casts doubt on other savings institutions, which soon find themselves besieged by depositors. There then results wholesale bank dumpings of mortgages and government securities on the market, in order to raise cash to pay their depositors. Among other things this fire sale of bonds drives up interest rates sharply.

Corporate stocks are then dumped because the yields from bonds are considerably more attractive and because expectations have turned downward and panic is beginning to set in. The stock market tumbles badly daily, and major corporations, seeing the way the wind blows, begin to retrench on their investment plans, cut down on inventory accumulations, and trim their work force. Laid-off workers reduce their current purchases sharply and begin to default on their installment credit and mortgage payments. With rising defaults, financial institutions undergo a second relentless wave of pressure and liquidation, with the weaker of them going bankrupt. At this point, the country is well into a major financial and economic crisis.

In opposition to the apocalyptic picture I have painted, the conventional wisdom places its faith in the ability of government to prevent any such denouement for the sick society. The prevailing faith among both liberals and conservatives is that government, using Keynesian (and/or Milton Friedman's) economic theories, can save the day. Why, then, do I believe Keynesian economic policy unlikely to meet the kind of economic challenge discussed above?

One problem is that the existing widespread belief in the infallibility of government support, which has by now percolated down to most business groups, in itself increases the likelihood of an eventual economic crisis. Believing the government cannot and will not "allow" a breakdown, individuals and firms have embarked on far more risky courses than they would have considered acceptable even in earlier boom periods.

As a result, while the need for curbing rapid inflation is seen by virtually everyone, actually doing it has proven to be far more difficult than anticipated. One possible route, a major cutback in government spending, has come up against the fact that military spending, in Vietnam and elsewhere, accounts for the bulk of the federal budget. Cuts in these expenditures are strongly resisted by the foreign policy makers for fear of weakening the U.S. empire abroad by bringing into play the "domino effect." Moreover, the most alienated and dangerous sectors of the population are demanding more rather than less government spending in nondefense areas.

This leaves monetary policy as the chosen government instrument for curbing inflation. The efficacy of this approach, however, is limited by the fact that monetary policy aims at curbing inflation essentially by limiting the growth of the money supply. Underlying this approach is the classical "quantity theory of money," which starts with the definition that the economy's total annual output, in money values, is limited to the amount of money supply (quantity) times its "velocity," i.e., how many times the money supply turns over during the year. The heart of monetary theory is the belief that the velocity of money is relatively constant over the years. If this is true, then curbing the money supply should curb the total output of the economy, usually by some combination of reductions in real output and prices.

One trouble with this approach is, as we have seen, that the tremendous postwar growth of liquid assets outside the money supply proper has enabled individuals and businesses to continue increasing their purchases even though the money supply is held constant, or even declines slightly. Thus, they can sell government bonds or corporate bonds or stock in order to get cash. Ultimately, this must reflect the fact that the velocity of money is not constant, but has increased in recent years, i.e., people are using the existing supply of cash plus checking accounts more efficiently, and turning them over more quickly than before. Recent studies have shown this to be just the case. According to one survey by economist J. Daniel Khazzoom, "All of these point to the same conclusion—the notion of stability of velocity in the face of changing money supply is not warranted."

While the increasing velocity of money makes it more difficult for the government to curb inflation, the gravest problem lies in the opposite direction. The inescapable fact is that over the last twenty-five years paper monetary values have increasingly gotten out of line with physical reality—and the classic capitalist solution is deflation, more commonly known as depression, which destroys some of these paper values to restore the balance. Even David Bazelon, who argues in his analysis of the U.S. economy, *The Paper Economy,* that "The Federal government has underwritten the Paper Economy—and the underwriter will not permit a really effective deflation," also states:

The Paper Economy is like a balloon, which is why the key terms are inflation and deflation. . . .

We have not yet figured out a workable substitute for the ritual of bankruptcy and other forms of price reduction and deflation—for letting the air out of the balloon.

By tightening the monetary supply sufficiently, a point will be reached at which an offsetting increase in its velocity will not be possible, and inflation will end. The end of inflation, as necessary and inevitable as it may be, however, threatens far worse effects for the economy.

For one thing, paradoxical as it may seem, the end of U.S. inflation could seriously aggravate the international monetary crisis. This is due to the enormous nongovernmental European holdings of "Eurodollars," which are simply dollars loaned to banks outside the United States, primarily by Europeans. One key to the U.S. ability to weather the 1969 financial storm was that the extremely high rates paid by U.S. banks for borrowing these "Eurodollars" effectively spirited huge sums away from the treasuries of European governments; since only foreign governments can demand gold from the United States in exchange for dollars, this greatly lessened the pressure on the U.S. gold supply. (In the first six months the total supply of Eurodollars jumped by 50 percent, to $40 billion, largely in response to the increase in Eurodollar interest rates from 7.5 percent to over 11 percent.) Unfortunately for the United States, most of these Eurodollar loans are very short term (three months or less). The great danger is that since a successful end to U.S. inflation will undoubtedly reduce interest rates all over the world, many of these Eurodollars may return to European governmental treasuries, which in turn may be tempted to convert them into gold.

The direct domestic effects of ending inflation could be even more disastrous. A reduction in production that is likely to attend the slowdown in inflation is normally closely associated with higher unemployment; in fact, higher unemployment is generally seen as one key to slowing inflation, since it would provide a deterrent to labor demanding increased wages. (Underlying this view is a variant of Marx's surplus industrial army theory, which held that a pool of unemployed labor effectively prevented wages from going up.) The trouble today with unemployment as an inflation cure is that it involves political and social dynamite. In particular, the fact that blacks normally are the first to be laid off when unemployment increases creates a dangerous situation. The powers that be are clearly aware of this, as indicated, for example, in the statement of a top executive of Bethlehem Steel Corporation, criticizing the idea of ending inflation by wage-price controls:

. . . if the present Administration will take a statesmanlike enough attitude, and stand firm, and slow this thing up until you've got 7 or 8 percent unemployed—I'm not recommending it, I'm just saying "if"—I think it would be a more effective retardant action than the other [controls]. But it's political suicide. The crux of the problem now, I think, is the impact of a given increase in the over-all unemployment figure on the blacks.

This was not a problem that we had in the Korean war or in World War II, or at least if it was, nobody recognized it.

A similar point has recently been made by the U.S. government in discussions with foreign officials, according to *The New York Times*:

Central bankers from the United States have told their Western European and Japanese counterparts that the United States cannot accept the social cost implicit in getting rid of the balance-of-payments issue.

The most effective way to eliminate the payments deficit is by prescribing a recession, but the Americans argue that the first men to be laid off, according to traditional employment patterns, would be unskilled black workers. This, they say, would produce an intolerable aggravation of racial disquiet.

In addition, ending inflation by cutting production and income raises a related danger that is largely ignored in current economic thinking. As we have seen, those most up to their necks in debt are young workers and blacks, the same alienated groups who normally would be most likely to be laid off during a recession. As economist Sylvia Porter aptly put it: "In short, in trouble will be those least able to find their way out of trouble." Furthermore, if the purchasing power of these groups declines, the resulting reduction in demand for goods produced by other sectors could further spiral the economy downward.

Assuming, as I do, that the government will of necessity succeed in slowing inflation, the final and crucial question is, "What can it do to prevent a subsequent major depression?" The government tools available for fighting a depression fall into two general (and overlapping) categories: preventive measures, particularly in the monetary sphere, aimed at generating confidence and preventing panic (manipulating the monetary supply, insuring bank deposits, etc.); and curative measures, particularly in the expenditure area, aimed at maintaining consumer purchasing power (public works programs). Part of the problem to date with the confidence-generating preventive measures is that as we have seen they have engendered overconfidence, making the cure, given an initial shock, even more difficult.

In addition, the enormous growth in the postwar period of liquid assets outside the direct control of the government has greatly weakened its influence in this area. At the end of World War II, households, nonfinancial businesses, and all banks together held 44 percent of their financial assets in the form of U.S. government securities. This meant that at that time any threatened liquidity crisis could easily be counteracted by the federal government, since close to half of these assets were federal debt that the government could in effect redeem for cash. By the end of 1968, these same groups held only 9 percent of their assets in government bonds, which severely limits the government's liquidity-creating powers. Put another way, a 25 percent drop in the stock market would now *wipe out* more assets of these groups than the federal government could make liquid by repurchasing *all* their U.S. government bonds. In any event, monetary experts generally agree that with confidence down during a deflationary period, monetary policy is of limited value, being likened to "pushing on a string," i.e., you can lead the horse to the bank but you can't force him to borrow.

Finally, a basic weakness of expenditure measures is that they are generally slow to be undertaken, needing a recognition of their necessity, congressional approval, etc. Even the awareness of being in a dangerous economic situation is delayed by the lag in collection of key statistics, as well as their frequently poor quality. In the view of one who should know, assistant Budget Bureau director Maurice Mann, the economic data being used for making crucial government policy decisions are so weak that "we are playing 'Russian Roulette' with our economy." Monetary crises and panic, on the other hand, wait for no man and spread like wildfire. Furthermore, the very process by which the government would use Keynesian theory to stimulate investment and employment—massive deficit spending or increasing the money supply—can itself lead to the erosion of private sector confidence in its own future, and to a further decline in private economic activity.

In the last analysis, the government theoretically could

overcome these problems by hiring, directly or indirectly, so many workers that it would effectively take over all economic activity. Such a step, of course, would mean the end of the capitalist system as we know it. However, the chaos and distress caused by the severe deflation itself would undoubtedly generate such political instability that it is difficult to forecast an ultimate outcome. What we do feel certain of, however, is the validity of the prediction of one radical economist, Jacob Morris, that "one of the casualties of this crisis will be the Keynesian theory of the crisis-proof monetary management of the capitalist economy."

PART IV

PROSPECTS FOR THE PATIENT

8

PROSPECTS
FOR THE PATIENT

American society is beset by two sets of diseases. The first is the chronic illnesses of continuing overseas involvement, racism, and alienation. The second, even more threatening to our current society, is the serious monetary afflictions, both at home and abroad. The crucial question is, what are the likely prospects for the patient's progress?

In my view the sick society's chronic illnesses are not remediable within the anatomical framework of the present corporate-dominated society. Economic expansionism abroad is vital to the key corporations that dominate the economy, and is likely to be a continuing source of conflict with both developed and underdeveloped countries alike. Black poverty appears virtually insoluble since the corporate sector's single-minded devotion to profit maximization prevents it from generating the strong pressure necessary to overcome the political power of local groups with a vested interest in racial discrimination. Alienation is basic to a dog-eat-dog competitive society where profit is the driving force and human considerations must take a back seat.

Even the development of automation, which is now in its infancy, and has a long road to travel before it can free mankind from the need to toil, can not heal the corporate society—indeed, it could well turn it into a nightmare. If we imagine a society where robots could produce all goods (including themselves), it might appear that since people could not work to earn a living goods would have to be given away. This could mean a society of abundance but one without profits and hence corporations as we know them. Fortunately for the longevity of today's corporate sector, even under total automation there is always likely to be a range of desirable services uniquely performable by humans in conjunction with material assets: teachers and schools, doctors and hospitals, actors and theaters. Through advertising and social conditioning many other services, however intrinsically valueless or perverted, can be transformed into "needs" of people. Under these conditions, "service" corporations can hire these workers and profitably control the sale of their output. Moreover, as long as a substantial service sector exists, goods-producing corporations can still prosper by selling their automated output to the service workers. Thus, the corporation can still retain its function and power in society.

To take an extreme example, I can envision a corporate society where control over other people's lives becomes an inculcated "need" of all individuals. People would then work five days a week as "slaves" of others in order to earn the money to hire others as such slaves in their nonworking time. A handful of monopolistic giant slave corporations, with the capital and organization to rent slaves of the desired brands and types would control the supply and demand. They could thus generate profits that would accrue to the upper 1 percent of the population owning these corporations, allowing this elite to buy 20 percent of the slave services of the country. Overseas entanglements, involving control over foreign slaves, racism, and alienation, would all be natural elements of this corporate society.

While this may seem a farfetched vision, the fact is that as goods production requires ever less labor, and goods consumption tends to move closer toward satiation, the big corporate sector as a whole is already moving into the service area. Right now this involves entry into such areas as leisure and recreation, health, and the "knowledge industry." The relative shift from goods into services takes place in two ways. One is the faster than average growth of big firms specializing in these areas, e.g., Polaroid or Hilton Hotels. The other is the increased entry of big goods-producing corporations either through new ventures or acquisitions, e.g., big oil companies build motels and big electronics corporations buy up book publishers. Since this trend is clearly established, even automation appears to be no barrier to the corporate sector's continued domination of society.

In my view, moreover, the chronic illnesses of the sick society are not necessarily fatal. Given the nuclear detente among the world's big powers, continuing American expansionism and struggle for control of foreign countries need not inevitably lead to the sick society's physical destruction, although this is a grim possibility. While the black minority can cause considerable damage insofar as its struggle for equality turned violent, it is hard to believe that the corporate society does not have the power to suppress it, through force and/or co-option. Although alienation may be a more widespread problem, in its most virulent and dangerous form it affects only a relatively small group, principally minorities, intellectuals, and students.

As I have noted, the "silent majority," or more accurately the passive majority of middle-age white America, suffers from alienation generated by the sick society's economic system. But, subjectively this alienation is not experienced as sharply by them as by the minorities described. For one thing, the majority is preoccupied with earning a living (a living that is not very high by absolute standards and which is very low compared to the American dream—or even that level reached by most intellectuals). For another thing, the majority, which lives with grim memories of the Great Depression, can now truly feel it has "never had it so good." Third, the majority has been successfully sold a bill of goods by the educational system and the mass media as to the indisputable greatness of America —the land of two cars and thirty-six months to pay. Finally, because it is a majority that conforms to the demands of society's leading institutions. "Middle America" does not experience the persecution that the minorities do. In fact, Middle America can safely displace its aggressions by being the persecutor. It must be remembered, however, that these aggressions themselves ultimately are generated by the inescapable alienation inherent in American society.

Moreover, it should also not be forgotten that even Middle America is not a fixed group, but rather a collection of individuals at varying stages of the life cycle. Even if in their mature years they come to realize the inadequacies and injustices of the corporate society, the most likely response is not collective political action but individual attempts to allow their children to "do better" in life, e.g., by saving money for college educations. Thus, their children have to learn their own lessons each time and may well not learn them before it is too late and they too seek salvation only for their own children.

Hence, normally it is only the dramatic economic breakdowns such as the 1930s Great Depression, which really galvanize the energies of Middle America toward directions of a more fundamental change. At those times it is not some vaguely felt alienation or malaise that is troubling them and can be covered over by mass entertainment and looking to one's children. Rather what is at stake is their very livelihood—their ability to provide food, clothing, and shelter for themselves and their children, and their maintenance of a position of dignity in their own community. It is at this point, when people feel desperate, and are unemployed and have time to think and act, that the corporate society is truly in danger.

Thus, as long as the economy can be prevented from collapsing, while the sick society may operate at below par and be vastly deficient in human terms, it could live on for many decades, if not centuries. The really serious threat is the crippling economic breakdown, the likely causes of which were discussed in the last two chapters. This would be a death by heart attack, owing to the failure of the system's blood—money—to circulate through the social body.

In growing but still murky recognition of these potential dangers, the last few years have seen "Doctor Government" trying to minister to the patient. Inevitably, however, the prescribed treatment has vacillated. Attempts are made to cool the inflationary fever of the patient and the threat of a run on the dollar by "bleeding him"—i.e., restricting the circulation of money. Because of the inevitably uneven results of this treatment less healthy parts of the body begin to turn moribund, and the government panics. It then attempts to inject a monetary adrenalin into the patient. An obvious example of this pattern was the Federal Reserve Board's increasing of the money supply following the near panic caused by the 1970 bankruptcy of the Penn Central Railroad—a bankruptcy that was helped along by the original tight money policy. All the while, however, the patient's psyche, as measured by business and consumer confidence, inevitably deteriorates as a result of the increasing uncertainty, the trauma of sudden failures, and the shifts of direction.

Therefore, while the chronic ills of the system are not necessarily fatal, other than in terms of the human spirit, the picture becomes very different if we add to it the likely heart attack of an economic breakdown. Thus, Daniel Moynihan's preinaugural memo to President Nixon, which stressed the role of an expanding economy in the 1960s in preventing social breakdown, noted that, "If a serious economic recession were to come along to compound the controversies of race, Vietnam, and cultural alienation, the nation could indeed approach instability." In my view a major economic collapse, as opposed to simply a "serious economic recession," would mark the end of the corporate society as it now exists.

One reason is that an economic collapse would furnish the final deathblow to modern liberalism, which in its broadest sense is the ideology of the corporate economy. Liberalism provides not only the means of supervising the overall economy but also a perceptual apparatus for viewing reality. In addition, it holds out to most groups a putative answer to the sick society's problems and the promise of its eventual cure. To understand in what way liberalism plays these crucial roles, and why it would collapse along with the corporate economy, we must first look at its early roots as well as at its historic role in post-1929 America.

Every modern ideology normally serves several functions, including providing an intellectually and emotionally satisfying explanation of reality as well as a vision of the road to a better society. Liberalism is no exception. Its rise in eighteenth-century England can be seen partly as a response to the stifling of economic development under the bonds of medieval feudalism. The core of early liberalism was individualism. Thus, Adam Smith expressed liberalism's belief in the efficacy of free markets to transform the selfish actions of individuals into the progressive and good economy. Similarly, John Stuart Mill saw democracy as the means by which free, rational men, increasingly educated, could have progressive, good government.

In the United States, partly as a result of the Great Depression, liberalism's belief in economic individualism came to be modified, with a need seen for democratically controlled government to redress the sometimes errant workings of the market economy. This was connected to humanistic concern for the underdog, e.g., workers, blacks, aged. In the area of foreign relations, liberalism hoped for an extension of American democracy abroad, and was strongly antifascist and anticommunist.

As such, American liberalism has some glaring weaknesses that have been eroding its influence in the last decade. For one thing, society is not just a collection of individuals, but is divided into classes and groups. Moreover, as I have tried to show, the upper-income class has not only dominant economic power but also very great political power. The failure adequately to take this into account is one reason that liberalism cannot offer a good explanation of increasing American expansionism abroad. The myth of defending freedom against tyranny has worn increasingly thin as the United States involves itself deeper and deeper in defense of tyrannical puppets in underdeveloped countries—particularly in Indochina.

Liberalism also fails to explain why the world's richest democracy cannot eliminate black poverty. Its emphasis on gradual change through rational means tends to obscure the fact that force, or the threat of force, buttresses every society, including ours, and is usually necessary for radical change. Thus, just as liberalism rejects the need for revolutions abroad to destroy the powerful forces that have held back development, it fails to see why blacks at home cannot be satisfied with attempts at rationally persuading their fellow men to give them a share of the good life.

Moreover, the liberal emphasis on individualism runs counter to emerging new strains of communalism, particularly among youth. Thus, liberalism does not offer a satisfactory emotional philosophy for the increasing numbers of alienated people who reject individualism and private corporate profit making in favor of communalism and public egalitarianism.

All these weaknesses partly reflect the white middle-class bias of American liberalism. Slow change can be acceptable to liberals because as a group they are quite economically, politically, and socially successful. Related to this, there tends to be a strong streak of paternalism among liberals, who want to do things for the underdog rather than give him the power to do it himself. These attitudes often seem reenforced by a subtle bourgeois–Puritan belief that liberals are really a superior people (the "elect" of Puritan England) who deserve their higher position in society. Thus, on an emotional level, American liberalism, which successfully overcame the conservative view that "I am not my brother's keeper" with the golden rule philosophy to act toward my fellow man as *if* he were my brother, is now under challenge from the radical belief that I have a duty to my fellow man because he *is* my brother.

One of the most prominent characteristics of contemporary liberalism is its relative ineffectiveness in the great debates and struggles now taking place. Liberals have inveighed ad nauseum against the increasing "polarization" of society, a trend that to a certain extent represents the increasing perception of underlying divergences of interests. But, by and large, liberals have failed to come up with a trenchant analysis of the problems that face us, let alone viable solutions. One senses that liberalism has "tired blood" and even an air of mustiness as its prescription for our ills boils down to more and more of the "New Deal."

Why is this so? For one thing, liberals are rationalists, and as events increasingly contradict their view of the world, this tends to put them in intellectual disarray. On top of this, liberalism is a philosophy of an older generation, which cannot face that their whole view of America is based on myths—that in fact America *is* an oligarchical, imperialistic, racist, sick society. It is easier to cling tenaciously to the belief that recent horrendous history, such as the Indochina war, is an accidental phenomenon that will disappear and be replaced by steady progress. Finally, as older rationalists and intellectually oriented individualists, liberals tend to have great difficulty dealing with emotions. Hence, it is difficult for them really to comprehend the surge of communal feeling that has developed among the young and that challenges prevailing beliefs and institutions, from the glories of the nuclear family to the wisdom of universities.

The one as yet unchallenged tenet of liberal faith is the

belief that beneficent government, using Keynesian medicine, has solved the fundamental economic problem of stability. This belief provides the base for liberalism's dream that as the economic pie steadily grows bigger and bigger, government can take larger and larger slices to redistribute to minorities and social investment in general. Continuing economic growth has thus become the keystone of liberal hopes for slow but steady social progress. If then, as I believe, an economic collapse will completely destroy this blind liberal faith in governmental powers over the economy, it would provide the *coup de grace* to liberalism as a viable ideology.

The immediate result would be an enormous vacuum, both in terms of ideology and power. What is certain is that this vacuum will not last long. For one thing, the unwillingness of people to suffer prolonged periods of unemployment and economic depression without demanding strong governmental action to get the economy rolling again clearly differentiates the present era from that of the 1930s. Given this, the only two political forces that logically would contend to fill the vacuum are some type of "state capitalism" and some variant of socialism. In what follows I speculate upon the prospects for each of these two "cures" for the sick society.

By "state capitalism" I mean a system in which government would attempt to revive the collapsed economy through widespread direct intervention, while generally leaving ownership of the corporations in the hands of their stockholders. Government would attempt to overcome the fundamental weakness of the capitalist economy—the lack of coordinated decision making—by substituting its presence for the invisible hand. One can speculate at length on the possible governmental measures that could be taken to restore employment and production. These could include reduced taxes and greatly increased federal spending, government loans to business, and even in some cases government take-overs of key firms or industries.

In theory, such governmental action could go a long way toward reviving, temporarily at least, a collapsed economy. In practice, however, there would undoubtedly be enormous difficulties. The principal problem would be to find profitable outlets for the vast quantity of goods that can be produced under full employment. For one thing, federal spending normally is highly concentrated and stimulates directly only a handful of industries in the economy. Moreover, after the shock to confidence caused by a collapse, both business and consumers are likely to be very cautious and emphasize saving over spending. Finally, since state capitalism leaves both ownership and profits in the hands of the small minority who cannot spend their income, it will not overcome the present system's consistent tendency toward underconsumption and hence overproduction relative to market demand.

What little historical experience we have with true state capitalism suggests the road such a society might take. The most prominent case is Nazi Germany, which succeeded in reducing unemployment from six million to one million in four short years after Hitler came to power. However, this success lay primarily in the development of a repressive society based on a war economy. One great "virtue" of such an approach from the standpoint of state capitalism is that all military output is purchased by the government and there is no difficulty in providing profitable outlets for defense industry production. Thus, the easiest way to restore a collapsed economy under state capitalism is to hire millions of the unemployed as soldiers and use other millions as producers of military goods. An additional advantage is that such a war economy provides military demand for consumer goods for soldiers, as well as the correct psychological atmosphere for getting the civilian sector to accept the necessary sacrifices.

In theory, since there is no necessary link between state capitalism and authoritarian repression, the German nightmare need not be the model for American state capitalism. There seems, however, little reason for optimism on this score. An economic collapse will require quick and decisive government action on the part of the state capitalists in order to maintain corporate power at home and abroad. At the same time, the polarization of American society insures that there will be resistance to a state capitalist solution. Those who resist are likely to be blamed for causing and/or prolonging the crisis, thus serving as the scapegoats for justifying repression.

The ideological elements that could lead to this brand of authoritarian and repressive state capitalism in America as a response to an economic collapse are already numerous. There is clearly a fairly large group of Americans who believe in the myth of America as a just society, where those who work hard get ahead, and whose main error has been continually to extend a helping hand to the inferior and ungrateful at home and abroad. The corollary of this world view is that the good society is threatened both by external forces of communism and internal agitators influenced by foreign ideologies. These agitators reject the American dream because they are themselves unsuccessful and cannot compete, and they appeal to similar types. Blacks and other minorities, intellectuals and hippies, who clearly have never "met a payroll" are the worst offenders. Insofar as they have not accepted the basic legitimacy of

American institutions and have created general social upheaval—perhaps thereby causing the economic collapse—
it would be necessary to crush them in order to restore and
maintain the good life.

Such a "philosophy" would appeal most to poor, unedu-
cated whites, particularly those of relatively recent rural
backgrounds who long for the simplicity of bucolic America; to parts of the middle class, particularly white-collar
workers who believe in an ordered life; and to some elements of the business sector, like the Texas oil millionaires
and the war goods corporations that require shrill patriot-
ism for expanding business. A major economic depression,
particularly one triggered by a monetary collapse and a
crisis of confidence, could easily lead these groups to feel
that repression and authoritarianism would be necessary
to restore a stable society. Additionally, such an economic
collapse could make state capitalism of an authoritarian
kind appeal to many more people from all walks of life because something drastic clearly would be required to restore their economic and psychological equilibrium.

More significantly, a major economic breakdown could
make state capitalism particularly appealing to the dominant section of the ruling corporate elite and upper class.
At present it is far more efficient for the corporate society
to have a liberal democratic government, where even the
talents and labor of the disaffected, particularly intellectuals, can be harnessed without massive overt coercion.
Such a liberal society, which fits in well with American tra-
ditions, is also far more useful for winning foreign influence. But, threatened by the alternatives of continuing
stagnation at a low level, or a sharp turn to the radical left,
the corporate sector as a whole would undoubtedly opt for
saving its privileged position through state capitalism, of

whatever degree of authoritarianism and repression required. This is true even though there is no historical evidence to show that such a system could last very long—witness Hitler's vaunted "thousand year civilization" that destroyed itself in a dozen years.

The only other fundamental cure for a stricken society would be its reorganization along the lines of collective public ownership, or socialism. Right now the constituency for such a society would appear to be quite small, consisting largely of some students and intellectuals and black and minority militants. But it is hard to say what groups might be won over to such a society under the crisis conditions of an economic collapse. This depends, in part, on what form of socialism is offered as an alternative American way of life.

In theory there are many possibilities, ranging from a highly authoritarian and centralized socialist society to a very democratic and widely decentralized one. Practically speaking, my own view is that if socialism is ever to have a chance to replace and heal the sick society, it will have to be quite different from any type now functioning elsewhere in the world. The core of a successful American socialism would have to be determined by the highly developed U.S. economy plus the need to win over the great majority of Americans to this socialism before the new society can be born. The great majority will be needed because the forces favoring state capitalism will have great power in the interregnum of the vacuum. At a minimum, the managers and wealthy of the corporate world, along with much of the governmental bureaucracy, and particularly the armed forces and police, would favor state capitalism rather than socialism. In order to neutralize some of these elements and win over a vast majority of others, the

of coordination required to meet these goals. Such planning is necessary if for no other reason than to analyze and take into account all social costs and benefits of given economic activities. No longer would it be thought conceivable to simply value a chemical plant on the basis of its profitability without taking into account the cost of pollution that it generates in the environment.

On a more general level, coordinated planning is needed to develop rationally and carry through the enormous reconstruction of a society that has grown haphazardly and on the basis of distorted priorities. Not only is there a need to strike a better balance between collective and private consumption, but also between making resources available for future generations versus consuming them now. As we have seen, the corporate society has a built in bias toward short-range plundering and a calculated disregard for long-run repercussions. To overcome the heritage of this approach will require a great deal of investment and construction—in housing, schools, hospitals, recreational facilities, rebuilding our decaying cities, and developing new ones. By its very nature such wide-scale and long-term construction and investment requires equally comprehensive planning if we are not to end up with a hodgepodge of wasteful activity.

Coordinated planning also will be necessary if the socialist society is to meet its humanistic responsibility for drastically revising our treatment of oppressed groups at home and our relations with other countries abroad. In both cases this should start with a recognition of the fact that for far too long the sick society used its enormous power to gain at the expense of others, and a moral debt has accrued that is now payable on demand. Moreover, how such a debt is to be repaid is something that should not be decided unilaterally, but rather with the active participation of those who have been wronged.

Thus, with regard to black people and other oppressed groups in America, it is not sufficient simply to legislate against discrimination of all kinds. What justifiably may be demanded are subsidies and preferential treatment for jobs, education, and housing in order to redress the inequities that have accumulated over the centuries.

In the international sphere a reversal is needed in the present net outflow of resources from the underdeveloped countries to the developed ones. This is a special obligation for a country with 6 percent of the world's population that uses half of the world's resources. In the short run the main American aid to the underdeveloped economies could come through one simple step: withdrawing our economic, political, and military support for the tiny ruling elites in the underdeveloped countries who have helped us to block change in order to preserve privileged and profitable positions. In addition, the United States should renounce all its overseas investment and the special privileges such as military bases which have buttressed this investment. All of our foreign economic relations have to be constructed anew, on mutually agreeable bases. To help redress the injustices of the past we should also offer technical and material assistance on a vast scale, in the forms which the underdeveloped countries choose for starting on their own paths of development. One logical step is for American farms, which are incredibly productive but now restrict output in order to maintain high prices, to be operated at full capacity (a situation normally achieved only during major wars), with the surplus shipped abroad to needy countries.

From the preceding discussion of some of the basic

principles of a healthy socialist society one potentially grave problem may be apparent. Namely, given the high degree of economic planning and coordination postulated, the danger would be that those who run the economic apparatus would have the keys for political totalitarianism. Overcoming this danger is one of the major structural problems American socialism would have to solve.

Somehow ways must be found to give individuals genuine participation in and control over the basic institutions of society, including not only all formal levels of government but also schools, hospitals, farms, factories, and offices. Toward this end a great deal of experimentation is going to be needed in ways of defining and developing "community" or "local" control of key areas of life. But, even if totalitarianism were not a danger such a search would be necessary if people are genuinely to determine their own destinies.

While specifying the answers to this problem will be a difficult task indeed, no useful solution can result from throwing out the baby of a coordinated economy with the bathwater of political authoritarianism. A decentralized economy, with worker ownership of individual factories, as for example Yugoslavia has, inevitably in my opinion will lead to many of the defects of the present sick society. These include a lack of coordination that can lead to major depressions, as well as a drive for profit maximization that can lead to widespread alienation. Thus it is necessary to concentrate on mechanisms for allowing genuine individual participation and local control while still retaining the advantages of a relatively centralized and planned economy.

It should be clear that if the principles of such a society could be put fully into practice, we would take a long stride toward healing the illnesses of the sick society. Since the basic propelling force of American militarism and intervention abroad is the corporate sector's drive for profits, its elimination would abolish the strongest bases of America's unhealthy foreign involvement and allow us to become a truly "good neighbor." Destroying the economic roots of racism would not only allow black economic progress, but might gradually erode the virulent prejudices associated with the depressed position of blacks in American society. These steps, along with the elimination of the profit motive as the overriding criterion for economic decisions, would go a long way also toward eliminating alienation and discontent; so too would the new possibilities for genuine individual participation and for channeling energies into altruistic behavior both here and abroad.

Whether it is possible to achieve such a healthy socialist society depends on many factors and developments in the years ahead. But it seems to me that a vital prerequisite is the recognition that the present corporate capitalist society is dying from fundamental diseases, and is not just experiencing a temporary lapse of health. If, following an economic collapse, state capitalism takes over we can be certain that it will not cure the society's chronic ills, but will in fact worsen them. Since the new system is likely to be predicated on militarism, it will increase our aggressive foreign interventions, and at the same time generate increasing discontent at home. Insofar as it will be based on repression and intolerance for minorities and intellectuals, the problems of black poverty and alienation will be further aggravated.

One grave danger is that if authoritarian state capitalism does get a foothold in America, it could destroy our society as well as the rest of the world by military aggressiveness and miscalculation. Even if it did not wreak such horror, for however short a period it lasts, such a system would make the night fall on America. My hope is that a clear understanding of our basic problems and alternatives in the coming years will help us to avoid this night and proceed directly to the dawn of a healthy society.

NOTES

235

be seen from a few illustrative numbers. For a company that seeks an average profit of 15 percent per year on its investments, $1.00 in profits earned two years from now is worth only 72 cents today; this reflects the fact that at a 15 percent rate of interest compounded annually 72 cents grows to $1.00 in two years. By the same logic, $1.00 in profits earned 10 years from now is worth only 20 cents today, and $1.00 earned 20 years in the future has a present value of only 4 cents. (At the higher percentage rates of profit sought by many corporations, the present value figures shrink even more rapidly with the passage of time.) Hence the corporation's relative indifference to long-run effects when making its current decisions.

14-15   John Kenneth Galbraith, *The New Industrial State* (Boston: Houghton Mifflin, 1967); discussion of sources of economic power, pp. 56–58; definition of techno-structure, p. 71.

15-16   Leonard S. Silk, "Business Power, Today and Tomor-row," *Daedalus,* vol. 98, no. 1 (Winter 1969), pp. 181–2; emphases in original.

18   Goldston, "New Prospects for American Business," p. 82.

19   Computation of changes in *Fortune's* top "500": *The New York Times,* March 3, 1969, sec. 3, p. 1.

20   Data on income of companies and corporate management are from annual reports and proxy statements for 1969.

20   Milton Friedman, *Capitalism and Freedom* (Chicago: The University of Chicago Press, 1962), p. 133.

20   Adam Smith, *The Wealth of Nations* (New York: Mod-ern Library, 1937), p. 14.

21   Judson Gooding, "Blue-Collar Blues on the Assembly Line," *Fortune,* July 1970, pp. 69–70.

23   *Economic Report of the President, 1969* (Washington, D.C.: Government Printing Office, 1970), p. 175.

23-24   Michael Harrington, "Why We Need Socialism in Amer-ica," *Dissent,* May–June 1970, p. 244.

25   National Commission on Urban Problems, *Building The American City: Report 1968* (Washington, D.C.: Gov-ernment Printing Office), p. 275; as quoted in Harring-ton, "Why We Need Socialism," p. 243.

CHAPTER 2

28   Woodrow Wilson, *The New Freedom* (New York: Doubleday, 1913), pp. 57–58.

29   Nicholas Johnson speaking on the Dick Cavett Show, ABC-TV, August 25, 1969; quoted in *Monthly Review,* November 1969, p. 11.

30   Julius Klein case: Jack Anderson, *Washington Exposé* (Washington, D.C.: Public Affairs Press, 1967), pp. 33–34, 194–96.

31-33   My discussion of the historical corporate-government relationship, including the quotations, draws on: Edwin M. Epstein, *The Corporation in American Politics* (Englewood Cliffs, N.J.: Prentice-Hall, 1969), pp. 20–41.

34   Alexander Heard, *The Costs of Democracy* (Chapel Hill, N.C.: University of North Carolina Press, 1960), p. 119.

34-35   Direct corporate contributions: Epstein, *The Corporation in American Politics,* p. 93.

35-36   1956 campaign contributions: Heard, *The Costs of Democracy,* pp. 114–15; data on 1968 campaign contributions from *The New York Times,* April 20, 1970, p. 52; quote from Epstein, *The Corporation in American Politics,* p. 95; 1964 campaign contributions: Richard J. Barber, *The American Corporation* (New York: E. P. Dutton, 1970), p. 199.

36   Information on Textron and Ford executives from *Wall Street Journal,* October 16, 1968, p. 1. Advertisement for Humphrey-Muskie in issue of October 25, 1968, p. 14.

38-39   Data on the Business Council, and quotations, from Hobart Rowen, *The Free Enterprisers: Kennedy, Johnson and the Business Establishment* (New York: Putnam, 1964), pp. 61, 74, 88, 96, 280, 204.

39   On corporate occupancy of cabinet posts: C. William Domhoff, *Who Rules America?* (Englewood Cliffs, N.J.: Prentice-Hall, 1967), p. 97.

40   Corporate officials in the Nixon administration: Barber, *The American Corporation,* pp. 196-97.

40-41   David Horowitz, with David Kolodney, "The Foundations," *Ramparts,* April 1969, pp. 47–48; characterization of Council by Douglass Cater, *Power in Washington* (New York: Random House, 1964), p. 247.

41-42   Drew Pearson and Jack Anderson, *The Case Against Congress* (New York: Simon and Schuster, 1968), pp. 103–5, 119.

43   1956 campaign data: Heard, *The Costs of Democracy*, pp. 114–36.

43   Representative Bennett quoted in Robert Sherrill, "We Can't Depend on Congress to Keep Congress Honest," *The New York Times Magazine*, July 19, 1970, p. 7.

44   Senator Robertson: Pearson and Anderson, *The Case Against Congress*, pp. 195–96; Sherrill, "We Can't Depend on Congress," p. 22.

44   Defense contractors and congressmen: Pearson and Anderson, *The Case Against Congress*, pp. 343–44.

45   Senator Fulbright: Pearson and Anderson, *The Case Against Congress*, p. 417.

45   Epstein, *The Corporation in American Politics*, p. 128.

45   Julius Klein: Pearson and Anderson, *The Case Against Congress*, p. 396.

45   Millionaire U.S. Senators: George G. Kirstein, *The Rich: Are They Different?* (New York: Tower Publications, 1970), p. 159.

45-46   Senator Kerr: Pearson and Anderson, *The Case Against Congress*, p. 136.

46   Senator Long: Sherrill, "We Can't Depend on Congress," p. 6.

46   Congressmen and banking: Pearson and Anderson, *The Case Against Congress*, pp. 186–87; Sherrill, "We Can't Depend on Congress," p. 6.

47   Congressman Byrnes: Sherrill, "We Can't Depend on Congress," p. 22.

47   Congressional holdings of radio and television stations: Pearson and Anderson, *The Case Against Congress*, p. 181.

48   Corporate communications to public officials: Epstein, *The Corporation in American Politics*, p. 99.

48   Joseph Clark, *Congress: The Sapless Branch* (New York: Harper & Row, 1964), pp. 20, 113.

49   Congressional reform legislation: Anderson, *Washington Exposé,* pp. 48–50.

49   Nixon and the ABA: *The New York Times,* July 28, 1970, p. 1.

50   Domhoff, *Who Rules America?,* pp. 109–11.

50   On regulatory agencies as original creatures of the corporations, see Gabriel Kolko, *The Triumph Of Conservatism* (Chicago: Quadrangle Books, 1967). For a summary of the metamorphosis theory see Epstein, *The Corporation in American Politics,* p. 83.

50-51 Lee Loevinger quoted in Domhoff, *Who Rules America?,* p. 108.

51   Client-controlled regulatory agencies: Epstein, *The Corporation in American Politics,* p. 217.

51   Ritchie P. Lowry, *Who's Running This Town?* (New York: Harper & Row, 1965), p. 25.

52   Richard Holton, "Business and Government," *Daedalus,* vol. 98, no. 1 (Winter 1969), p. 58.

53   Daniel Bell, "Notes on the Post-Industrial State," *Public Interest,* Winter 1967, p. 30.

53   Data on universities: James Ridgeway, *The Closed Corporation* (New York: Ballantine Books, 1969), p. 2.

53   Data on foundations; Hearings before Subcommittee No. 1 on Foundations, Select Committee on Small Business, House of Representatives, 88th Congress, Second Session, *Tax-Exempt Foundations: Their Impact on Small Business,* July–September 1964, pp. 3–5.

54-55 Data on corporate-university interlocks: North American Congress on Latin American, *Who Rules Columbia?* (1968); Africa Research Group, *How Harvard Rules* (1969); Ridgeway, *The Closed Corporation,* p. 23.

56   Ridgeway, *The Closed Corporation,* p. 8; emphasis added.

58   *Wall Street Journal,* March 25, 1969, p. 19; see also *The New York Times,* March 9, 1969, sec. 3, p. 1.

58-59 Barber, *The American Corporation,* pp. 177–79. It might be noted that while ultimately the government allowed LTV to take over Jones and Laughlin, part of the agreement was that LTV had to sell off two of its major acquisitions, Braniff Airways and Okonite Company.

59-60   On Leasco Data Processing and Chemical Bank: *The New York Times,* February 19, 1969, p. 65, and February 21, 1969, p. 62; *Business Week,* April 26, 1969, p. 144.

CHAPTER 3

63-64   Arthur M. Schlesinger, Jr., "A Middle Way Out of Vietnam," *The New York Times Magazine,* September 18, 1966, sec. 6, pt. 1, p. 47.

64-65   Ronald Steel, *Pax Americana* (New York: Viking Press, 1967), pp. 15–18, 320.

67   U.S. businessmen and the CIA: *Wall Street Journal,* February 24, 1967, p. 1.

67   Standard Oil of New Jersey: its foreign investment from 1969 *Annual Report;* on comparative number of overseas employees, Richard Barber, *The American Corporation,* p. 20; on intelligence-gathering reputation, Carl Marzani, *The Survivor* (New York: Cameron Associates, 1958), p. 294.

67   On the two-way flow of personnel between the oil industry and government: Robert Engler, *The Politics of Oil* (New York: Macmillan, 1961), pp. 310–12.

69   Trade data from International Monetary Fund, *International Financial Statistics,* April 1970; investment data (for new plant and equipment) from U.S. Department of Commerce, *Survey of Current Business,* September 1970.

69   Harry Magdoff, *The Age of Imperialism* (New York: Monthly Review Press, 1969), pp. 173–202.

70   Magdoff, *The Age of Imperialism,* p. 178.

71   Earnings and profit data from *Survey of Current Business,* October 1970; earnings include (a) earnings on direct investments abroad, (b) fees and royalties on direct investment transferred to parent companies in the U.S. and (c) income from "other" investments (other than direct) transferred to U.S. owners of these assets.

71   Capital goods sector: Magdoff, *The Age of Imperialism,* pp. 188–91.

72   Clarence B. Randall, *The Communist Challenge to American Business* (Boston: Little, Brown, 1959), p. 36.

72-73   Imports of strategic raw materials: Magdoff, *The Age of Imperialism*, pp. 50–52.

73   1957 investment data: U.S. Department of Commerce, *United States Business Investments in Foreign Countries* (1960), p. 144.

73-74   Gabriel Kolko, *The Roots of American Foreign Policy* (Boston: Beacon Press, 1969), pp. 16–26; quote on p. 17.

75   Harry Magdoff, "Militarism and Imperialism," *American Economic Review,* vol. LIX, no. 2 (May 1969), p. 237.

75-76   Senator Dirksen's list: *Congressional Record: Senate,* 91st Cong., 1st sess., 1969, vol. 115, no. 103; reprinted in the *Guardian,* March 7, 1970, pp. 14–15.

76   Eliot Janeway, *The Economics of Crisis* (New York: Weybright and Talley, 1968), p. 65.

76-77   Investment data: Victor Perlo, *American Imperialism* (New York: International Publishers, 1951), pp. 123–24.

77   Dean Acheson quoted in David Horowitz, ed., *Corporations and the Cold War* (New York: Monthly Review Press, 1969), pp. 124, 96.

77-78   Jordan and Welch quoted in Perlo, *American Imperialism,* pp. 122, 129.

78-79   John Loftus, "Petroleum in International Relations," *U.S. Department of State Bulletin,* vol. 13 (August 5, 1945), pp. 173–75; emphasis added.

79   Leo Welch quoted in Engler, *The Politics of Oil,* p. 267.

79-80   Howard K. Smith, *The State of Europe* (New York: Alfred Knopf, 1949), pp. 83, 205.

80   Marshall quote and Horowitz comment in: David Horowitz, *The Free World Colossus* (New York: Hill and Wang, 1965), p. 88.

80   Will Clayton quoted in David Horowitz, ed., *Corporations and the Cold War,* p. 164.

81   Marshall Plan agricultural exports: Perlo, *American Imperialism,* pp. 150–51.

81   Marshall Plan oil imports: data from Engler, *The Politics of Oil,* pp. 219–20; my profit estimate.

81-82   Marshall Plan and oil refineries; Perlo, *American Imperialism,* pp. 157–58.

82   Comparative economic growth rates for 1950–60 for real
        gross national product: U.S. Department of Commerce,
        Bureau of the Census, *Long Term Economic Growth:
        1860–1965* (Washington, D.C.: Government Printing
        Office, 1966), p. 101.

82-84   On the Iranian situation see: Michael Tanzer, *The Politi-
        cal Economy of International Oil and the Underdeveloped
        Countries* (Boston: Beacon Press, 1969), pp. 321–26.

83-84   David Wise and Thomas B. Ross, *The Invisible Govern-
        ment* (New York: Random House, 1964), p. 110.

84-86   This account of Guatemalan events based largely on
        David Horowitz, *The Free World Colossus,* pp. 163–
        186; information on drafting of oil laws in English from
        Eduardo Galeano, *Guatemala: Occupied Country* (New
        York: Monthly Review Press, 1969), p. 54.

85-86   Miguel Ydigoras Fuentes' statement from his *My War
        with Communism* (Englewood Cliffs, N.J.: Prentice-Hall,
        Inc., 1963), pp. 49–50, quoted in Horowitz, *The Free
        World Colossus,* p. 184.

87   Anthony Eden, *Full Circle* (Boston: Houghton Mifflin,
        1960), p. 647.

87   New York *Herald Tribune* and State Department reports
        in Horowitz, *The Free World Colossus,* p. 191.

87   *The New York Times* report and Engler comment in
        Engler, *The Politics of Oil,* p. 264.

87-88   Dulles statement: C. Wright Mills, *The Causes of World
        War Three* (New York: Simon & Schuster, 1958), p. 66;
        emphasis added.

88   Kassem overthrow: Horowitz, *The Free World Colossus,*
        p. 192.

88   Wise and Ross, *The Invisible Government,* p. 139.

89   *Wall Street Journal,* June 24, 1959, p. 1.

89   *The New York Times,* quoted in Harvey O'Connor,
        World Crisis in Oil (New York: Monthly Review Press,
        1962), pp. 261–62. For a more detailed analysis of the
        Cuban oil events see Tanzer, *The Political Economy of
        International Oil,* pp. 327–44.

89-90   *I. F. Stone's Weekly,* April 1, 1963, p. 2.

90   Data on U.S. investments and profits: U.S. Department of Commerce, *Survey of Current Business,* October 1970.

91   Senator Neely quoted in: Bahman Nirumand, *Iran: The New Imperialism in Action* (New York: Monthly Review Press, 1969), p. 65.

91   Chase Manhattan Bank's Vice-President quoted in Magdoff, *The Age of Imperialism,* p. 176.

CHAPTER 4

94   Black-white poverty comparisons: income data (for 1968) from U.S. Department of Labor, Bureau of Labor Statistics, *The Social and Economic Status of Negroes in the United States, 1969* (Washington, D.C.: Government Printing Office, 1970), p. 24; housing data (from 1960 Census) in John F. Kain, ed., *Race and Poverty: The Economics of Discrimination* (Englewood Cliffs, N.J.: Prentice-Hall, 1969), p. 113.

94   Gabriel Kolko, *Wealth and Power in America* (New York: Frederick A. Praeger, 1962); Michael Harrington, *The Other America* (New York: Macmillan, 1962).

95   On abolition of poverty: J. N. Morgan, M. H. David, W. J. Cohen, and H. E. Brazer, *Income and Welfare in the United States* (New York: McGraw-Hill, 1962), pp. 3–4, as quoted in Paul Samuelson, *Economics: An Introductory Analysis,* 7th ed. (New York: McGraw-Hill, 1967), p. 121.

96   "Transcript of Nixon's Address to Nation Outlining Proposals for Welfare Reform," *The New York Times,* August 9, 1969, p. 10.

97   Harrington, *The Other America,* p. 25.

99   *The New York Times,* April 29, 1968, p. 16.

99-100 George Sternlieb, *The Tenement Landlord* (New Brunswick, N.J.: Rutgers University Press, 1966), particularly pp. 93, 146, 223; Chicago data reported in Alan Batchelder, "Poverty, the Special Case of the Negro," *American Economic Review,* May 1965, p. 531; data on percentage of black incomes spent on housing from U.S. Department of Labor, Bureau of Labor Statistics,

Consumer Expenditures and Income, Urban United States, 1960–61, supplement 1 to BLS Report nos. 237–38 (April 1964); aggregate black rental housing expenditure estimated assuming urban black income of about $30 billion in 1970.

101   NAREB reversal: *The New York Times,* November 14, 1968, p. 79.

102   Donald H. Bouma, "Analysis of the Social Power Position of a Real Estate Board, "*Social Problems,* Fall 1962, pp. 121–32; Donald H. Bouma, "The Legitimation of the Social Power Position of a Real Estate Board," *The American Journal of Economics and Sociology,* October 1962, pp. 383–92; quotation, p. 391.

102-3   National Association of Real Estate Boards, State Associations Committee, *Forced Housing Kit,* February 1964, mimeographed.

103-4   On real estate board alliances: Bouma, "The Legitimation," pp. 388–89; on the public housing referendum, Bouma, "Analysis of," p. 124.

105-8   Data for this discussion of public housing drawn from Leonard Freedman, *Public Housing: The Politics of Poverty* (New York: Holt, Rinehart and Winston, 1969); his summary on pp. 6–7; Taft quote, p. 176; Abrams' quote, p. 164.

108-10 Data on ghetto merchants: David Caplovitz, *The Poor Pay More: Consumer Practices of Low Income Families* (New York: The Free Press of Glencoe, 1963); quotes from pp. 19, 29.

109   Federal Trade Commission Study reported in *The New York Times,* July 26, 1969, p. 30.

112   Edward F. Cox, Robert C. Fellmeth, and John E. Schulz, *Nader's Raiders: Report on the Federal Trade Commission* (New York: Grove Press, 1970), p. 56.

114   Kenneth Clark quoted in Arjay Miller, "Business with a Social Conscience," *The New York Times Book Review,* January 18, 1970, p. 8.

114-16 Georges F. Doriot, *The Management of Racial Integration in Business* (New York: McGraw-Hill, 1963); quotes from pp. 10, 11, 8; emphasis added to latter.

116-17   Lee Berton, "Slum Renovation: The Profit is Elusive," *Wall Street Journal,* June 11, 1969, p. 18; Mrs. Gabel quoted in same article.

117   Jules Cohn, "Is Business Meeting the Challenge of Urban Affairs?" *Harvard Business Review,* March–April 1970, p. 69.

117-18   *Fortune,* January 1968, pp. 131, 202.

118-19   *Report of the National Advisory Commission on Civil Disorders* (New York: Bantam Books, 1968), pp. 558–69.

119   On critique of NAB data: *Business Week,* May 16, 1970, p. 29.

120   Laurence O'Donnell, "In Motown, Caution Proves Successful," *Wall Street Journal,* July 11, 1969, p. 8.

120   On the impracticality of saving jobs for hard-core unemployed at Ford: *Wall Street Journal,* April 14, 1969, p. 12.

120-21   Comments of Whitney Young and Saul Alinsky from William Serrin, "At Ford Everyone Knows Who Is the Boss," *The New York Times Magazine,* October 19, 1969, p. 142.

121   *Wall Street Journal,* July 11, 1969, p. 8.

121-22   *Barron's,* July 29, 1968, p. 1.

122   *The New York Times,* April 11, 1970, p. 62.

122-23   Black domestics: Jack Minnis, "How the Great Society Solves the Servant Problem," *Life with Lyndon in the Great Society* (Newsletter), vol. 1, no. 6, reprinted in Marvin E. Gettleman and David Mermelstein eds., *The Great Society Reader* (New York: Vintage Books, 1967), pp. 168–70.

123-24   The MESBIC Program: *The New York Times,* June 29, 1970, p. 1.

124-26   On EG&G's Roxbury venture: *Wall Street Journal,* July 3, 1969, p. 10; *Business Week,* January 31, 1970, p. 107; *Wall Street Journal,* April 1, 1970, p. 12; *Fortune,* May 1970, p. 74.

126   James L. Sundquist, "Jobs, Training and Welfare for the Underclass," in *Agenda for the Nation,* Kermit Gordon, ed. (Washington, D.C.: Brookings Institution, 1969), pp. 57–58.

126-27   Earlier history of black capitalism: Earl Ofari, *The Myth
          of Black Capitalism* (New York: Monthly Review Press,
          1970), pp. 30–41.

127   Jules Cohn, "Is Business Meeting the Challenge of Urban
          Affairs?," p. 69.

127   *Wall Street Journal,* December 24, 1969, p. 1.

CHAPTER 4 (EPILOGUE)

129   *The New York Times,* August 5, 1963, p. 10.

130   Response to Chock Full's help-wanted ad and report of
          picketing: *The New York Times,* August 8, 1963, p. 13.

131   Data on William Black's philanthropy: *The New York
          Times,* May 8, 1964, p. 44.

131   Quote on Columbia: James Ridgeway, "Columbia's Real
          Estate Ventures," *The New Republic,* May 18, 1968,
          p. 15.

132   Quotes from William Black: on Columbia Business
          School, *The New York Times,* December 14, 1964, p.
          43; on efficiency, *Forbes,* June 15, 1962, p. 38.

132-33   On Chock Full store in Wall Street: *Wall Street Journal,*
          September 24, 1969, p. 1.

CHAPTER 5

136   Data on income distribution: Herman P. Miller, *Rich
          Man, Poor Man* (New York: New American Library,
          1964), p. 52.

138   Psychological warfare leaflet: *World Journal Tribune,*
          January 5, 1967, p. 2.

138-39   "MACE" letter: *Guardian,* January 20, 1968, p. 2.

139   Tobacco industry: Murray Kempton, *New York Post,*
          quoted from *Consumer Reports,* January 1968.

140-41   Drug industry: Drew Pearson and Jack Anderson, *New
          York Post,* February 6, 1968.

141   Vance Packard, *The Waste Makers* (New York: Pocket
          Books, 1963), particularly pp. 40–44.

142   Ruth West, "The Care and Feeding of the Very Rich," *McCall's,* August 1969, pp. 57, 109.

143   Marketing consultant Victor Lebow quoted in Packard, *The Waste Makers,* p. 21.

143-44   Edwin H. Sutherland, *White Collar Crime* (New York: Holt, Rinehart and Winston, 1961), pp. 17–28.

144   Ferdinand Lundberg, *The Rich and the Super-Rich* (New York: Lyle Stuart, 1968), pp. 118–19.

144   Data on cost of crimes in 1968: Edward E. Cox, Robert C. Fellmeth, and John E. Schulz, *Nader's Raiders: Report on the Federal Trade Commission* (New York: Grove Press, 1970), p. 194.

144   On the advertising industry see Vance Packard, *The Hidden Persuaders* (New York: Pocket Books, 1958).

145-46   Sutherland, *White Collar Crime,* pp. 235–36.

146   *Oil and Gas Journal,* February 20, 1967, p. 29.

146-47   Reader response to Albert Z. Carr's "Is Business Bluffing Ethical?" *Harvard Business Review,* January–February 1968, quoted in *Wall Street Journal,* June 20, 1968, p. 16.

147-48   On corporate management: Vance Packard, *The Pyramid Climbers* (New York: Fawcett World Library, 1964), pp. 18–21, 38, 78, 117, 162, 226.

148   Sutherland, *White Collar Crime,* p. 236.

148   Packard, *The Pyramid Climbers,* pp. 241–42.

149   C. Wright Mills, *White Collar* (New York: Oxford University Press, 1951), p. xvii.

149   Sales manager quoted in Packard, *The Pyramid Climbers,* p. 211.

149   Sutherland, *White Collar Crime,* p. 236.

149-50   Psychologist's approach to motivating salesmen: *New York Post,* February 15, 1968, p. 68.

150   *Wall Street Journal,* April 9, 1968, p. 3.

151   Exchange between Senator and editor: Clark Mollenhoff, *Despoilers of Democracy* (New York: Doubleday, 1965), p. 1.

151-52   On Senator Dirksen: Lundberg, *The Rich and the Super-Rich,* p. 510.

152   Senator Long: Lundberg, *The Rich and the Super-Rich,* p. 719.

152   Joseph Clark, *Congress: The Sapless Branch* (New York: Harper & Row, 1964), p. 22.

152   Paul Powell case: *Wall Street Journal,* January 14, 1971, p. 1.

153   *The New York Times,* December 26, 1966, p. 23.

153   Lundberg, *The Rich and the Super-Rich,* p. 518.

153   James Ridgeway, *The Closed Corporation: American Universities in Crisis* (New York: Ballantine Books, 1969), p. 11.

154   On universities and motivational research, see Packard, *The Hidden Persuaders,* pp. 23–24, 213; advertising executive quoted on p. 223.

154-55 Spokesman for TV writers: *The New York Times,* March 23, 1968, p. 63.

155-56 TV producer quoted in Packard, *The Waste Makers,* p. 192; emphasis added; chairman of Allied Stores, p. 61; General Foods official, p. 189; Valentine's Day commercialism, p. 142.

156   Dristan ad: *The New York Times,* October 27, 1968, Sec. 4, p. 6.

156   Desire for additional income: Packard, *The Waste Makers,* p. 146.

156   Man on the moon: *Fortune,* October 1970, p. 73.

156-57 Black concert pianist: *The New York Times,* January 3, 1968, p. 64.

157   Professor on child-conditioning: Packard, *The Hidden Persuaders,* p. 136.

159   Herman P. Miller, *Rich Man, Poor Man,* p. 54.

160   *Business Week,* October 10, 1970, p. 100.

CHAPTER 6

167   *The New York Times,* November 22, 1968, p. 73.

168-69 Data on United States balance of payments and gold holdings from various issues of *Federal Reserve Bulletin;* data on U.S. foreign investment from various issues of *Survey of Current Business.*

170   French Foreign Trade Secretary: *Wall Street Journal,* February 24, 1966, p. 7; emphasis added.

171   *The Economist* (London), February 5, 1966, pp. 527–528; emphasis added.

172   Data on foreign holdings of gold and total reserves at end of 1969: International Monetary Fund, *International Financial Statistics,* April 1970. 1969 data are not distorted by 1970 issuances of SDRs and "hot money" flows.

172   Jean Servan-Schreiber, *The American Challenge* (New York: Atheneum, 1969), p. 3.

177   William McChesney Martin, Jr., quoted in *Wall Street Journal,* September 15, 1970, p. 5.

178   *Business Week,* November 1, 1969, p. 38.

179   On a "United States of Europe" see George Ball, *The Discipline of Power* (Boston: Little Brown, 1968).

181   *Wall Street Journal,* April 4, 1968, p. 3.

183   *Wall Street Journal,* November 22, 1967, p. 33.

184   European government economist quoted in *Wall Street Journal,* March 18, 1968, p. 6.

187   IMF economist quoted in *Wall Street Journal,* November 18, 1968, p. 19.

CHAPTER 7

189   Hillel Black, *Buy Now, Pay Later* (New York: William Morrow, 1961), pp. 86, 177.

192-93   Aggregate debt and liquid asset data: Board of Governors of the Federal Reserve System, *Flow of Funds Accounts: 1945–1968* (Washington, D.C.: Federal Reserve System, 1970).

192   Corporate liquidity data cited in *Monthly Review,* September 1970, p. 7.

193-95   Family debt and stock ownership data: *Survey of Consumer Finances: 1967* (Ann Arbor: University of Michigan, Survey Research Center, 1967).

196-97   M. Carter McFarland, "Major Developments in the Financing of Residential Construction Since World War

II," *Journal of Finance,* May 1966, p. 384, emphasis added.

197   Banking institutions' assets and liabilities: *Flow of Funds Accounts: 1945–68;* data includes commercial banks, savings banks, and savings and loan associations.

197   Estimate of repayment obligations on home mortgage debt derived from calculations in *Monthly Review,* September 1970, p. 6.

198   McFarland, "Major Developments," p. 385.

199   *Wall Street Journal,* November 24, 1969, p. 1.

200   *Business Week,* November 15, 1969, p. 72.

204   J. Daniel Khazzoom: Letter to the Financial Editor, *The New York Times,* November 23, 1969, sec. 3, p. 17.

204-5   David T. Bazelon, *The Paper Economy* (New York: Random House, 1963), pp. 112, 106, 113–14.

205   Euro-dollar data: "Euro-dollars: A Changing Market," *Federal Reserve Bulletin,* October 1969, pp. 765–784.

206   Bethlehem Steel executive: *The New York Times,* November 23, 1969, sec. 3, p. 13.

206-7   Central bankers: *The New York Times,* November 18, 1969, p. 3.

207   Sylvia Porter, "Debt and Danger," *New York Post,* October 29, 1969.

207-8   Government bond data: *Flow of Funds Accounts: 1945–1968.*

208   Maurice Mann: *Wall Street Journal,* November 17, 1969, p. 40.

209   Jacob Morris, "Marx as a Monetary Theorist," *Science and Society,* vol. 31, no. 4, (Fall 1967), p. 420.

CHAPTER 8

218   Daniel Moynihan, "Memorandum to President Nixon" (January 3, 1969), *The New York Times,* March 11, 1970, p. 30.

228   United Auto Workers suggestion: *Wall Street Journal,* August 7, 1970, p. 19.

INDEX